SHE'S DOWNHILL AND IN THE SHADE

MEMOIRES INCLUDING THE MOST COLORFUL CHARACTERS AND EVENTS ALONG THE TRAIL.THE BOOK SPANS FORTY YEARS FROM THE GREAT SNOW MOUNTAINS OF THE GANG RANCH AND BRITISH COLUMBIA TO THE COWBOYS OF PENDLETON, OREGON.

Chris Kind
Ft. St. John, BC.
5 Aug. 2003

BOOK
BY

CHRIS KIND

Printed in Victoria, Canada

National Library of Canada Cataloguing in Publication Data

Kind, Chris, 1945-
    She's downhill and in the shade / Chris Kind.
ISBN 1-4120-0037-8
    1. Kind, Chris, 1945- 2. Outdoor life--British Colum-
bia--Anecdotes. 3. Outdoor life--Oregon--Anecdotes. I.
Title.
GV191.52.K56A3 2003   796.5'092   C2003-901372-3

TRAFFORD

This book was published *on-demand* in cooperation with Trafford Publishing.
On-demand publishing is a unique process and service of making a book available for retail sale to the public taking advantage of on-demand manufacturing and Internet marketing.
On-demand publishing includes promotions, retail sales, manufacturing, order fulfilment, accounting and collecting royalties on behalf of the author.

Suite 6E, 2333 Government St., Victoria, B.C. V8T 4P4, CANADA
Phone   250-383-6864   Toll-free   1-888-232-4444 (Canada & US)
Fax   250-383-6804   E-mail   sales@trafford.com
Web site   www.trafford.com   TRAFFORD PUBLISHING IS A DIVISION OF TRAFFORD HOLDINGS LTD.
Trafford Catalogue #03-0400   www.trafford.com/robots/03-0400

10   9   8   7   6   5   4   3   2   1

TABLE OF CONTENTS

Chapter one... The Gang Ranch
Chapter two...Trip to Pendleton
Chapter three........................ ....The Colts at Empire Valley
Chapter four...................There were Broncy Colts and there
                                        were Saddle Broncs?
Chapter five.............................Chilco and Gaspard Lake.
Chapter Six.....................................My best year in Rodeo.
Chapter seven............................Garry Powell Outfitting.
Chapter eight..................... .W.D. Dingler and R.G. Pierce.
Chapter nine.......................... Vold Rodeo and Jay Sissler.
Chapter ten..................................Back To Garry Powell's.
Chapter eleven.......................... ....The O.K. Ranch.
Chapter twelve.....................Cold Fish Lake & Hyland Post.
Chapter thirteen...........Creating the Spatzizi Provincial Park.
Chapter fourteen........................ Back to The Gathto River.
Chapter fifteen..............................The North lost a legend.
Chapter sixteen..The Muskwa.
Chapter seventeen..................Bighorns & The Fraser River.
Chapter eighteen...My Trapline.
Chapter nineteen.................................Ember and Bo.
Chapter twenty...................A most memorable hunt in Malta.

Introduction

The river was travelling quite fast, with swirling back eddies, its clarity was amazing and captivated you as the bottom moved so quickly underneath the small wooden boat.

My guide Polo did not speak a word of English, but was an expert at the oars and moved between the rapids like he was born on the river. Species of Birds that were all new to me were chattering back and forth. We drifted further; I was in a new world with sounds I had never heard.

The river was called the Tolten in central Chile, and something to behold. While I was admiring all the surroundings and beauty, wham! My fishing rod had a huge bend in it. The salmon was a beauty and gave me a good fight in the swift current. After fifteen minuets, I landed him.

My very good friend Orval McCormmach of Pendleton, Oregon invited me down to stay at his newly built home. His wife Candice was a native of Chile and their camp was situated 25 yards from the Tolten River. I like to say a camp, but in reality it was one of the most beautiful homes I have stayed in. The floors were wall-to-wall burls of natural hardwood, all meshed into a unique arrangement, sanded down and polished. The craftsmanship was superb. In the distance out there about twenty miles was the active volcano Villarica Vulcan It was while we were eating that salmon that I decided to start this book, something I had pondered for several years.

DEDICATION

I have known many a good Cowboy, Indian, Outfitter, Guide and Trapper along the trail. Not to mention several fine horses that I rode and quite a few that bucked me off. This book is a collection of events including all the fascinating characters that have been a major part of my life since 1962. I therefore dedicate this book to all those Good Hands that are still out there pumping air, and those Great Ones that are no longer here.

Wherever you are, I hope the hunting is good, and you are mounted on a fine horse. May your ride from here on out be down hill and in the shade.

When I was packing to leave home for the West, My Mother cornered me and said these words, "Though seldom practiced Christopher, there is no better system in all undertakings than to begin with the beginning". She was a smart person.

This is my story

She's downhill and in the shade

CHAPTER ONE

THE GANG RANCH

It was in the spring of 1962; the river looked bold and murky, the canyon it ran through was vast and majestic. It was a magnificent sight, the river was called the Fraser, and British Columbia, Canada was where this all happened. On the other side was the mightiest ranch in the world, the Gang Ranch. For a young lad just getting out of school, this was one of the most memorable moments. I new all my dreams were on the other side. Years of patiently waiting, 2nd thoughts of working with real cowboys and good horses would soon be a reality.

When I arrived in Clinton, I met three local cowboys. One looked like a pro football player without any shoulder padding. He was called Floyd Grinder and is a legend in the town. He was the first Indian I had ever met; the others were Jean Park and Henry Wai. These men are three of the finest outdoorsmen and cowboys, and after 40 years of sharing many a campfire I still consider them to be so. They took me out to the Pollard Guest Ranch, showed me how to milk a cow, and then I spent the night in the bunkhouse. I listened to their tales all evening on just what I was getting into and where I was heading.

I had one more day in town before I could catch the stage lines out to the ranch. I said goodbye to Floyd, Jean, and Henry. It would be two years before I would come to town and see them again.

I crossed that Fraser River on the Gang Ranch stage lines. Sid Elliot was the operator at the time. He was a fine gentleman who several years later became the mayor of the small town of Clinton.

Gang Ranch Suspension bridge over Fraser River

Any one going in or coming out could use the service. The mighty Gang Ranch was situated just a few miles from the river up on a high plateau. The Fraser River ran through the most spectacular canyon, with ridges covered in blue bunch grass. It was a sight to behold.

Several people were waiting for the stage line to arrive. All the supplies had to be unloaded into the store that the ranch operated.

I noticed a large man standing by the store; he had on a tan cowboy hat and looked like the boss. I finally met Mr Wayne Robinson the Manager of the Gang Ranch.

I think that from the way he looked at me, he was expecting a bigger person. I only weighed 85 lbs, probably thought I was wormy or something.

It was a very cold spring and still freezing at night. I had been officially given a position as chore boy. I had no idea what that meant, but sounded good to me. After many cords of split wood for the cookhouse, slopping the pigs, and whatever the cook wanted me to do, I figured out what my position was. I guess every green horn started the same way. At least I was on the ranch, living in the bunkhouse, and meeting all the hired men.

Gang Ranch Cook house and Bunkhouse

It did not take them long to realise just how green I was, they sent me on several errands to get left handed screwdrivers and chain pullers. It did not take me long to figure out when they were playing games.

I graduated to a more physical job as the spring progressed. That job was picking rocks out of the fields. I believe I picked all the rocks from one end of Bear springs hayfields to the other, all done with a stone boat. I know the piles are still there to this day. Each and every rock in those piles has my name on them.

One morning Wayne asked me to jump into the truck. We headed down to the bridge at the Fraser River. Standing at the bridge afraid to cross it was a young Pinto Filly. I do not know how he acquired her, probably at a sale. This was the first Paint horse that I had ever seen. Anyway he caught the filly right at the Fraser Bridge with a bailer twine. He made a makeshift halter out of it, and then he asked me to jump up and ride her back to the ranch bareback.

I didn't know that she was not broke. He hollered "just keep her on the road, not get her to excited, and hope for the best". He would follow behind with the truck. The filly went from a walk, missed the trot, and was into a fast gallop within seconds of me sitting on her backs. The next thing I knew we were flying up the road. I had a death grip with her mane as she rounded three sharp switchbacks and turned back to the river. She was supposed to turn right and go up to the ranch. Instead she turned left and headed back to the river at a much higher elevation. This definitely was not going down as planned.

We were heading for a very steep cliff. The filly went from a wide-open gallop to a dead stop as the edge of the steep bank in one stride. I went flying and rolled a hundred feet down the side hill right back to where I had started, the Gang Ranch Bridge.

Wayne came back down to the bridge with his truck, and asked me what happened. He laughed a little, and said " I thought you would have had her broke by now". I said something like I guess maybe, I did not get her broke in Three switchbacks or two minutes, whichever came first.

 I was pretty sore, but he found some humour in it. I guess he liked to see me in some kind of pain. Understandably so, he was a former United States Marine Sergeant.

 I was covered in cactus from head to foot and it took the cook at the ranch two days to pull them all out. From then on, everyone at the ranch called me cactus.

Wayne took me with him one day to Summer Range. We spent the whole day out along the banks of the Chilcotin River, looking the range over and dropping salt of. We went out onto the breaks of the Chilcotin and the steep canyons were right below. We found a shady spot and sat down and began to eat our lunch that the cook had prepared. Then we heard this loud roar and dust going up into the air like a volcano. What had happened was that just one ridge over; the whole side hill and bank slide into the Chilcotin River. This mountain for a period blocked of the entire river. We later found out, that it ruined that particular salmon run, and did a lot of damage to the fish ladders that were needed by the salmon to go up the river. Everything had washed away when the blockage finally broke loose. I could not believe how much of the mountain slid in to the river. If we had sat there eating our lunch on the one ridge over, we would not be here today.

Things were looking up; the cleaning of the barn became part of my job. It was huge, and held about thirty horses.

The Gang was still using a lot of teams to haul hay from the fields. One side was full of draft horses, and the other saddle horses. There were several excellent teamsters on the ranch. I remember Freddy Johnny; he used to start all the young draft horses, and had such patience and light hands with them. It did not take him long to get the young horses pulling like the older ones. He always hooked a young horse with an older one that knew what it was all about.

 Then there was Big Jim, I would watch him pick up bales in each hand and throw them as if they did not weight anything at all. To watch him eat at the dinner table was entertaining enough. He would eat two full plates of food maybe three.

There were about 400 to 450 horses on the ranch at the time I was there. One heavy stud horse was called Willy. He was a Sorrel Belgian and weighed in at 1700 lbs.

The other was a Chestnut Quarter horse called Sunny Bill, and another was called Picasso. I cannot remember Sunny Bill's breeding, but Picasso was a Hancock bred horse that I believe came up from Montana. He was one of the grandest horses I had ever seen. There was also a Blue Roan stud horse that was also of Hancock breeding, and belonged to Wayne.

 As summer came, I was promoted to haying and was given a team of horses to drive on a dump rake. My job was pretty simple, but I did not know anything about a team. The horses were terrible to drive. Every time I would step on the trip and dump the loose hay, it was a runaway. I would have fifteen to twenty runaways in the field every day. I was plumb scared of this one horse. The horse was called Chilcotin, and I literally did not have the strength to hold him. I will always remember his name. Somebody had to be at the ranch to help me unhook the horses, as I could not do it by myself.

One day there was a disaster. As I moved into the ranch, there was nobody there to help me hold the horses. I made a big mistake of trying to unhook the team by myself. I still do not know what happened exactly, but I did something wrong, they took off like scared jackrabbits, and I could not hold them. Down the road they went towards the ranch, pulling the dump rake wide open and full steam ahead.

 When they got directly in front of the Manegers house, they jumped the irrigation ditch and lost the left wheel on the dump rake. The axle hooked into the managers pretty white picket fence and pickets were flying everywhere like matchsticks. They went the full length of Wayne's picket fence, continued right through a wooden gate, lost the dump rake at the gate, and finally stooped at the barn.

I was shaking so bad, I thought I was going to die. Luckily Wayne Robinson was not there. Wayne was in town and would not be back for a few days.

The foreman on the ranch was a great guy by the name of Don Lower. Don was Wayne's son in law. He said not to worry, just get started cutting out new pickets and have them painted and in place before he returns. Don said if it is done right, he won't even know the difference. I worked all night and day trying to get it all in place before my funeral. I was plumb scared to death he would notice the difference.

48 hrs later, I had it all repaired and painted. When Wayne returned, I immediately told him that I had a small accident with Chilcotin, ˈbut everything was ok now. He replied that he understood the problems that I was having with the horse and let it go at that. I thought I was in the clear and felt relieved.

It wasn't ten minuets later that I heard this roar. I think something happened in my pants. He had a voice and the whole ranch heard him that day. Besides the fence, I had two full sets of harness that were in tatters and one wooden pole gate to repair.

I stood in front of him and listened to him tally the cost of all the repairs and damaged goods. I said that I would pay for all of the damages out of my wages. He replied, "that's right you will and at 90 dollars a month, you would be working for three years to pay for it all". I said that would be ok with me, but he never did dock my wages.

From then on someone was always there to help me unhook Chilcotin.

The next few days I tried to avoid Wayne, but that was hard to do because I had to report every morning to him for my orders. I longed for the days that I could take orders from the foreman. Everyone else did, but that was not so with me and never would be for a long time at the ranch.

I was asked to get Sunny bill ready to take to the lake ranch. He was to be turned loose with 30+ mares on the Bear Spring and Lake Ranch side hill. The mares were already out there; they had been rounded up and put in the pasture a few days before. My job was simply to deliver the stud to his pasture with his mares and turn him loose. The stud knew what this was all about, and was jumping all over the place.

I had a chain in this mouth and one through his halter and over his nose. That did not matter with him; his adrenalin was pumping and was already pretty high. That day I was riding a very old gelding. When we got to the lake ranch and he spotted all his mares, he jumped and bit me on my leg and held on. He bit me through my chaps, long johns, and right leg. I tried to pull his jaws loose, but he was too strong for me. I have marks to date from his teeth in my leg. I guess he thought he had a hold of the old gelding in his excitement.

There was no room for what he did in anyone's books and I was going to give him a lesson in some manners. There was one lonely tree at the lake ranch, I tied him up, and tried to teach him some manners, but I could not stand up. I was to late to teach him anything anyway, as ten minuets had already passed by then. All I wanted to do was to get rid of him in his pasture. He finally joined his mares. My leg hurt for weeks after that.

Even after what he had done to me, I could not really hold it against him. He used to stay cooped up for months on end, nobody would ride him and then all of a sudden one day, he has thirty girlfriends wanting him.

 It was not very many days later, maybe about a week or two, that I was to save the studs life. The butcher at the ranch was a man called Herb, who was from Nova Scotia. Herb had been a professional butcher in his day. He began doing all the butchering and meat cutting on the ranch, he also spent most of the day when not cutting meat irrigating the Lake Ranch fields. This area was all flood irrigated at that time. Herb used to ride an old gelding up to his fields and stake him near the meadow.

Sunny Bill was not that far away, he had spotted this gelding down in a field a half-mile away. He went down his fence line until he found a weak spot and jumped it. Then he went on down to the gelding, and intended to give him one heck of a butt kicking. Herb heard the wild commotion and went to his horses rescue. Herb was carrying a long 2x4 with canvas wrapped around it. He used to use it to put in a ditch for his irrigation and divert the water.

The stud had a hold of his gelding, and was not letting go. Herb hit Sunny Bill right behind the ear, and knocked him out cold as a cucumber. Being an old butcher, he knew exactly where to hit him.

A few others and myself were on horseback and had seen Sunny Bill racing down the side hill. It was luck that we were even in the area. We went at a gallop over the hills and when we got there, we saw Herb standing on the stud's head. He was pushing it down in the water that was flooding the field from his irrigation system. The stud was totally out cold, and if we had not been there, I know Sunny Bill that day would have met his demise. Herb was furious with the stud and meant business.

I jumped of my horse and held his head up. We then pulled his head around to get it out of the water. As tough and mean as he was, He was still the Ranch Stud and a very well bred one at that.

We took a halter off a horse and put it on him, then took him back to his pasture. He wobbled all the way up the hill, he looked blurry eyed and was coughing a lot of water when we turned him loose. Sunny Bill had no idea how close he came to meeting his maker that day.

Herbs' gelding was staked out at the lake Ranch all summer. The stud never again jumped his fence or bothered his old gelding. Herb said he would see him run up and down the fence line making all sorts of threats with his nickering, and stomping his feet, but that was as far as he got.

I rode Sunny Bill quite a few times after he returned to the Ranch. He needed lots of riding and was actually a pretty good old horse and not a bad cow horse. There were just so many good horses on the ranch that no one else would ride him.

One day when I was leading him out of the barn to his pen, he was nickering at a few of the horses as we went through the barn. Things a stud will normally do when there is a barn full of horses. When I reached the barn door, I turned to get his attention with the halter shank. When I did, I walked right into Mr Robinson who was coming in. It was like hitting a brick wall and so I jumped back. I said, "excuse me Mr Robinson you scared me". He grabbed me right by the throat, lifted me up against the barn door and said, "Let me tell you something one time you pigeon breasted sob, the day I do not scare you, you'll be going down the road". Then he put me down. He called me a lot of things, this pigeon breasted thing was getting real old, but I did not have the nerve to tell him that.

Myself and Sunny Bill at the Barn.

One evening at the Gang ranch store, when everyone was up there buying odds and ends, I approached the counter. Wayne was there with his wife serving the cowboys and ranch hands. I tried to quietly ask Wayne's wife to put a pack of cigarettes on my tab. She said, "what do you want, and to speak up so I can hear you". I did not want anyone to hear me, especially Wayne. He heard me repeat something and came over and asked what I wanted I mumbled something without looking him in the eye like I would like to buy a pack of cigarettes. His voice roared, He grabbed me in front of everyone in the store, lifted me up to the counter and said. "You want cigarettes, you want cigarettes, you cannot even suck fresh air let alone puff on these things. Don't ever ask for cigarettes in this store" He put me down and once again all the cowboys began to laugh. I don't know why, but he got a big kick out of lifting me up, and putting his face right into mine. At least that night in front of everyone, he did not use the phrase pigeon breasted.

I was asked to butcher a pig one day. I had helped Herb the butcher with a lot of beef and pigs and knew what to do. As I was preparing everything, a guy by the name of Pete walked by. He had just hired on and came from Montreal. Pete was a real street fighter and was quite a mean person. He asked to shoot the pig. I said ok, but to wait until he has his head in the slop pail and to shoot him in the right place. Pete got the 22 calibre and then kicked the pig in the nose. When he started running around his pen, he started to shoot the pig everywhere. He was hit in the shoulders and hams, and emptied the rifle and smiled. This guy had gone absolutely crazy. I dove over the fence when he started to shoot, for fear of getting a bullet myself. Once the rifle was empty, I surfaced and said to him "have you gone plum crazy"? When I reached for the rifle, he hit me and knocked me down. I left and went to see Wayne. Wayne told me that "you gave him the rifle, and that you were going to have to pay for the pig".

I had enough of this crap; I saddled a horse and packhorse, rolled my bedroll up and got some food from the cookhouse. I waited until dark and crept up into the bunkhouse and carried a full crate of coke bottles up the stairs and into Pete's bedroom. I figured about where his head was on his bed and smashed them as hard as I could down on him.

I ran down the stairs and jumped on my horse and galloped of into the dead of night. I was headed for the Bear Springs cabin. Wayne was looking for me everywhere. He finally found me up there. He said that he had fired Pete and it was ok to return to the ranch.

A few weeks later it was in the Vancouver paper that some longshoreman had killed Pete on the warf in Vancouver. This guy was mean and plumb crazy to boot.

My next job at the ranch was as a helper to a guy who came up from Montana. He had the patent to build the Beaver Slide. It was a loose Hay Stacker made with poles and wings. The loose hay was gathered with a Buck Rake and slide up onto the teeth of the Beaver Slide. It was then pulled up with a team of horses, or a piece of equipment and dumped over to make a stack. It was a great piece of equipment. The Gang put up a lot of loose hay back then. The ranch built three of them. Two went into use, while the third was never used. It sits there to this day and has never moved.

I was working more and more with horses and cattle, feeding calves and doing lots of sorting of stock around the main ranch. Wayne brought a heard of horses into the corrals, and cut out a fine looking four year old. He was a colt out of Sunny Bill, and was a bright Chestnut. I did not know what he was going to do with him, and then he told me to go and get my saddle and a hackamore. I ran to the barn and hurried to the corral before he changed his mind. This colt was just barely halter broke. The only ground work this colt saw, was me running to the barn. I felt pretty confident that I could ride him though, ground work or no. Wayne had him snubbed up to his Blue Roan Stud and told me to get him saddled and get on and not to waste his time about it, or he would change his mind. The colt was scarred to death, and I was shaking to. After I saddled him, I think both the Colt and I were more scared of Wayne and the Roan Stud than anything.

 He turned me loose in the corral with 50 other horses, he did not offer to buck at least not then, so he cut us out of the herd, opened the gate, and chased us out of the corral with a large stock whip. As we left, he shouted not to come back until suppertime.

The Colt went where he wanted to go, it was the blind leading the blind, and I was just along for the ride. Through the fields we went, we passed people haying and they would wave at me. When I waved back to be kind of friendly, he spooked and the race was on. Up side hills we went, and finally settled on a high ridge overlooking the ranch.

 I was scared to even move for fear he would buck me off, it was called something like "stealing a ride". The colt stopped on the ridge, scanned the horizon, and spotted about a 150 head of horses being driven to the ranch for sorting. Before I could even say, "here we go," In seconds he was in a wide-open gallop heading for the herd, tail in the air and nickering all the way. All I did was hang on. Into the herd we went and back to the ranch. When Wayne saw me in the middle of all the horses now entering the large corral, out came that large stock whip again and horses scattered everywhere. The colt and I both got it everywhere he could hit us. Then came the hollering, "I told you not to come back until suppertime." I was scared, the colt was scared, and neither one of us knew what to do.

The colt finally saw some daylight and wanted no part of Wayne Robinson. I shot out of the corral hanging on with Wayne on our butts. This time we did not come back until supper. He bucked me of many times that day, but when the sun finally went down, we were stuck together like glue. There was no way in the world this colt was ever going to leave my hands, or have anyone say that I gave up or could not get him broke.

I called this colt Copper; he was the first one I had ever started. At the end of the summer, he was going great and looking at cattle pretty well.

Myself and my first Colt "Copper"

I used to sit on the fence and watch all the cowboys working colts, they were great with a rope and could front foot them or rope them around their necks at will; they were so good at it. I said to myself I hope one day I can use a rope like they could.

Loren Wood on Gang Ranch Stud Sunny Bill and a young colt

The hands at the Gang Ranch were something to watch, there was Loren Wood, a cowboy from Oregon, Jack Shearer and the Cow Boss Marvin Guthrie, and that great cowboy Roy Williams. There was Don McDonald, Joe Auben, Walter Hurst, Ronnie Nichol, Walter Stobie and Johnny Jack. There was Willie Rosette, Joe Rosette, Mike Rosette and Ray. Isidor, James Kalelest, George Sergeant and Jimmy Harry. You could give anyone of these guys a young colt fresh of the mountain and watch them do a nice job. They could handle a rope and catch anything in or out of a corral. I watched them all, but the one that I learned so much from, was Loren. He was a master with a young horse and started

Marvin Guthrie and his lovely wife Pat

many fine young colts at the ranch. A few years later, he would invite me to Pendleton, Oregon to meet some Oregon Cowboys.

The one thing I watched and learned from all these guys was how to saddle and Pack horses so you did not sore them up. A horse that had a saddle sore was no use to anyone. These guys could go the whole summer riding horses without galling them.

It was early spring; a large horse roundup was to take place in the area heading up to the old Home Ranch. There were about ten good hands, all mounted on their best horses. I was so happy that Wayne told me to catch a certain horse called Crooked Nose and have him saddled. This horse would never have won a halter class, but was one of the finest cow horses on the ranch and he was now mine. Once a person is given a horse and he pulls his tail, he is your horse until you leave the ranch. I quickly pulled Crooked Noses tail to let everyone know where and to whom he belonged.

When we arrived at the area, Wayne was giving directions to everyone as to how he wanted to have this all done. I was told by Wayne to stay right with Roy Williams and not to ever let him out of my sight. Just as everyone was leaving, I noticed that everyone had a lariat on their saddle. I asked Wayne if I could have one also, he began to untie his own rope like he was going to give it to me, but instead he whacked me on the top of my hat and said "Listen you pigeon breasted sob you can't

even coil a rope let alone throw one, don't you ever ask for a rope until you learn how to coil one." I never asked him again about carrying a rope, but I did know how to coil one. I swore, if he ever called me pigeon breasted once more time, I would finally say something.

After several hours we came out into a small meadow, there were about 12 horses. It so happened they were the ones that were the most difficult to get in, as they had been running on the mountain for several years and yet to be corralled. Roy looked the difficult situation over and told me what he was going to do and the area he was going to herd them into. Roy told me that if anything happened and we were to get separated to head south, and if I hit the USA or Mexico, I had gone to far.

He was mounted on a fantastic horse that had been grain fed for the occasion and was as fit as a fiddle. It was a real privilege to even get to ride with Roy. Here I was on my first horse roundup, and with one of the best hands on the ranch all I had to do was keep him in sight.

Crooked Nose, the day after the roundup.

As soon as they saw us, the race was on. Roy hollered to stay with him. I guarantee you that I would have never lost him for anything. Crooked Nose was a fabulous horse to ride; he went through the timber like a Buck Deer. All I had to do was hang on; he would do the rest. After about two hours of the wildest ride through timber, creeks and draws, they gave up. We were able to get them lined out to our rendezvous place. When we arrived, there were a lot of horses at the fence line. When Wayne saw the ones that we were bringing in, he smiled and shook his head. I think it was the first time he had ever smiled at me.

That was all short lived, because I was back on his shit list the next day. It all happened at the Lake Ranch. Wayne was riding his best horse called Scar that he brought from Montana. Scar was a big and beautiful bay horse. He had excellent breeding and a very strong horse. We approached this irrigation ditch with water in it. I was riding Copper and we both eased up to the ditch. Scar was kind of looking for a place

Roy Williams and his lovely wife Red Cloud

Red Cloud and My Mother in 1964 at Williams Meadow cabin

to jump across, he was going to jump the ditch, but slightly hesitated for a moment. When I moved up along side of him, I stuck the toe of my boot under his tail for a little encouragement. Scar immediately jumped the ditch and flew to bucking. Gee wiz, I could not believe it. Scar was a 22-point horse at a rodeo that day, and you could have won Calgary on him.

I would have given Wayne a ten for his performance. Wayne hit the dirt hard and once he got his air, he screamed at me saying, "you stupid sob, you are fired for doing that, you are fired you stupid sob". I was quite surprised that he would react like that because he did it to me all the time that is sticking his toe in my horses bum. He could not wait for the opportunity

Anyway I started to ride off, and he hollered again saying," Where the hell are you going." I replied that you had fired me, and he said "go and get my horse you Pigeon breasted sob before I kill you". I sat on my horse and he then said, "Ok, I rehired you. I just rehired you back, now go and get my horse before I kill you"

One day soon after the horse roundup and this episode, Wayne called me up to his house, he said to pack my bedroll and head for Hungry Valley. After one year and a half at the ranch, I was finally going to cow camp with the boys, this was the moment that I had been waiting for all my life.

It was about fifty miles from the ranch to Hungry Valley. I was to overnight at Fosberry Meadow, and then ride the last fifteen miles over Blue Door into Hungry Valley. Copper was saddled this was all new country for him and me. I took Crooked Nose also. He had my bedroll and some grub on him. We left for the mountains and were finally on our way. Wayne explained the directions; we rode through Williams's Meadow and hit Gaspard Creek, then on up to the working corrals at Fosberry Meadow. There was a cow camp there and it was one of the main ones. Most all the cattle, some 13,000 head passed through that area. I cannot remember who was at that camp, but the cattle were already in the mountains, it was mid July.

Fosberry Meadow was lush with grass knee high to my horse. It stretched for several miles down to the Wales place, and could hold a lot

Willy Rosette and Myself in 1964

Myself on Sunny Bill

One of the Top Cowboys at the Gang Ranch and my good friend was Mike Rosette .He could ride with the best and sure could make a good Cow Horse. Mike now lives in a Log Cabin near Canoe Creek.

of cattle come fall time, when all the cows were heading home. I would later hold 1000 head on the meadow into January. I would spend months up with the cattle. It was two years before I even went to town. In the spring they started out towards Summer Range then on up White Creek to Gaspard Lake and Fosberry. There they rested a while and continued to Hungry Valley, Lost Valley, Graveyard Valley, and finally Relay. I took the first one hundred head of cows into Relay Creek. Never had that valley seen any cattle. It was like a new world and frontier opening up.

It was a very lush valley, the mountains were all around, and the Coast Range was not far away. The snow would come very early due to the elevation. We took a packhorse with salt to hold them for a few days. Later we were to bring a lot more salt on packhorses up to Relay Mountain. The cows stayed there all summer. It was up there, that I saw my first monster buck deer. He was well over thirty inches. I watched him for several hours and saw him day after day in the same spot. The area where the big bucks hung out was called Big Paradise and Little Paradise; they were two High Alpine Valleys of the main creek flowing into Relay Valley.

The next year Marvin Guthrie who was the cow boss had his father in law build a cabin in the Main Valley where Big Paradise Creek comes into Relay Creek. I believe it is still there to this day.

I remember skidding rails down of a hill for all the fencing needed and used to hold the horses. I had never rode a horse with a harness before, but it sure was the way to skid rails. I must have skidded rails for two weeks or so. There were a lot of logs for just about everything needed to make a good camp. From then on, more and more cattle filtered through Prentice Lake and over into Relay Creek. This was the opening of some country that had hardly ever seen any people and was sure pretty country with the mountains all around you.

The fishing in Relay Creek was real good and one could always catch supper with pan fryers.

Ron Nichol and Myself near Williams Meadow.

Joe Auben packing into Graveyard

Left to Right: Finest Indian Cowboys I have ever known
Mike Rosette, Jimmy Harry, Isidore Kaleleste, and Willy Rosette.
Taken at Bear Springs about the time of the Horse Roundup.

Churn Creek, The Big Basin, and The Little Basin. We tried to keep
the cattle out of this area in the late fall.

I remember several of us took just over 103 head of horses from the main Gang Ranch up to Big Paradise; it was over a hundred miles to the Snow Mountains. Jimmy 'Jiggs' Rosette held them there all summer. That was quite a ride for the first fifteen miles as we headed for Williams Meadow. We didn't loose any, but sure came close a time or two at Bear Springs.

Once we got a few miles on them, they settled down and moved at a lot slower pace. There was a young bay thoroughbred stud that Wayne bought from Slim Dorrin that was in the bunch. His job was to take care of the mares in the herd. Jimmy must have had a great summer. He was in simply some of the most beautiful country around and there were Snow Mountains everywhere.

As we moved the horses along Beaver Valley, I noticed huge Grizzly bear tracks coming down the valley. The creek crossings were all churned up with his tracks on each side. They were the largest I had ever seen, and would later in life see the same bear. He was as big and

black as an Angus Bull and weighed over a twelve hundred pounds; his name was Nero and was well known throughout the Gang Ranch.

Relay must have been the summer ground for most of the deer in the area; there were hundreds of them. Everywhere you looked, there was a big buck lying down on a ridge. Sometimes I would see several large bucks in one group. They were as fat as butterballs, all in the velvet. I know they sure liked the salt that I would put out for the cattle. As it turned out most every deer that wintered on the Fraser River and Churn Creek used to summer in the Relay's.

Marvin Guthrie the cow boss sure did a good job with keeping the cattle where they should be. He was a good man with a horse, knew cattle well, and always had a good cow dog at his heels; his dog's name was Bob.

To be the Cowboss on the Gang Ranch was a job that I sure would not want. It was so big and for anyone trying to keep track of all the cows in such a remote section of British Colombia was as far as I'm concerned a nightmare. There were valleys up in the back snow mountains that had never seen a cow. Not only did we have to move them around here and there, but we also had to watch for cattle getting into alpine valleys with bog holes and any toxic weeds. I used to like watching the dogs work. They would never give up, day after day; they were always there ready to go to work.

There were some great cow dogs in cow camp. All were raised on the ranch and all were Border Collies, one sure could move a lot of cattle with them through the brush and on over those High Mountain passes. I swear each one of those dogs could do the work of three cowboys. Sometimes I would send Yeller around the herd, and he would be gone for hours working his side of the cattle. Every once in a while, he would come over to within sight of me to check things out, and go back to his side. I did not even have to tell him where or what to do, he figured it all out by himself.

Don had Smokey and Dammit, Marvin had Bob, Joe had Rags, Willie had Gypsy and I had Yeller. With those six dogs, we could move several thousand head through the mountains.

Myself and Yeller in Hungry Valley

Myself crossing Big Creek in 1964 and in Hungry Valley with the dogs

Mickey hauling all our bedrolls and grub

One day we were all coming back from moving a thousand head or so over to Lost Valley. As we were returning to the camp at Hungry Valley, I noticed it was evening and the sun was going down. We were just a few miles from camp and we passed a small lake in West Churn. At the next pothole lake was a huge Grizzly bear drinking. We were all mounted on very good horses, and every guy there was good with a rope. Well you can figure out the next bit, we all got off, and reset our saddles and tightened them down while he had his head in the water. The next move was to cut the Grizzly off, which we did without any problem. When he saw us he stood up, it was then, that we realized we had disturbed a giant. He was a monster, as big as any Angus Bull the ranch had.

He now had a choice of swimming the lake, or facing 5 cowboys blocking him from the nearest point of timber. He chose the timber instead of swimming and started towards us. I thought wow this is great, peace of cake, and he's even coming to us. The only problem was that he was not the slightest bit afraid of us and was getting larger and larger every stride he took.

Nobody realized just how big this guy was or what we had bitten of until he was right on us. It is amazing how horses learn to side step perfectly when they want. In seconds they opened up a gap large enough for a freight train to go through, and it widened even further when the bear woofed at us when he passed by. He was huge and a Dark Silvertip. He was very close to a thousand pounds if not more.

I remember several cowboys throwing the loops on the ground, some in the air. Something they seldom did. All of them saying, "you get him, I missed". The sight of that flowing silky coat of hair as he went by is always in my memory. Sure glad we missed him because we would still be scattered up there in West Churn someplace picking up pieces of our saddles. There were some very large Grizzly on the ranch. They seldom if ever were seen. They were to smart for that and moved around at night. One could always see their tracks on the trails the next day as they passed from valley to valley. That summer, I saw two very large Grizzlies that went close to a thousand pounds their tracks measured from twelve to fourteen inches.

Joe Auben and Bob Livingston, two Gang Ranch Cowboys

´A few nights later, four of us were sitting at this little table in Hungry Valley cabin. There was an Indian called Jimmy Harry at one end of the table. While we were eating, a large packrat came through a part of the chinking and entered the cabin. Nobody moved to grab a rifle, because the rifles were near the beds several feet away. The rat jumped down to the floor and walked brazenly by the stove as we all watched. He was checking out our supper for the evening.

Jimmy slowly pulled out this large hunting knife and flung it at the rat. It pinned the rat to the floor. He calmly looked at us and said "you white men would not have taken this country so easy, if I would have been around that time". Someone replied. "Hell you don't even know how to sharpen a knife properly, let alone throw one. What you did was pure luck, if you can do that again I'll give you a months wages." He just smiled, and kept on eating his supper. Hell, I would have bet a month's wages also. I knew he could not pull that one off again. Jimmy stole the show that night

Hungry Valley in winter

Packing in to Big Meadow Cow Camp

Summer turned to fall, and cattle were streaming out of the mountains. It did not take those old cows long to figure out where the hayfields were when those first snow storms hit, they knew the trails well. It could snow in Relay and Lost valley in September quite often Cattle would drift into Hungry Valley and down West Churn to Big Meadows. We had to watch that they did not continue down Churn

Creek, as it could be hell to get them out once it got to icy. Others would drift over into Fosberry Meadow.

Before the herd was taken to the main ranch, we would sort the cattle and send some up to Big Meadow. Some one thousand head would remain in Fosberry and someone would hold them there into December and possibly January. I remember holding them there with Don McDonald and having Christmas and New Year in the small log cabin in Fosberry Meadow. It was one of the coldest winters on record. I do not know for sure how cold it was, but the horses had long pieces of ice hanging from their nostrils, and you could hear them walking on the snow a hundred yards away. We had to chop ice for the cow's everyday and move them back and forth across the meadow to break the snow down and expose the grass. When it was that cold, they did not want to come out of the trees. It was much warmer in the timber.

It was so cold some nights that the water was frozen in the cabin; we wondered if any cattle would be they're waiting for us in the morning. The cows would go into the thick spruce swaps. Then when the temperature dropped even more, we knew it would be impossible to hold them any longer and they streamed out for the ranch without even having to drive them. I remember moose were everyplace we looked. The cold had brought them down to the big meadows.

Once the cattle reached the Ranch, our job was then to do all the re-riding for lost cattle; sometimes a plane was brought in and cattle would be spotted. We would saddle and pack hay on the packhorses and of we would go, back into the mountains.

It was at that time that I met Chilco Choate. He said that he had heard I had shot four deer down at the ranch one summer and let me know that he was not very happy about it. He had the Outfitters Licence to Guide hunters in that area. I told him that it was quite normal for all the Native Indians and cowboys to live off deer. They had families to feed and often when I would return to the ranch, I would take something from the alfalfa field, and throw it over my saddle. It went to a good cause and every morsel was used including the hide. The hide was tanned to make gloves and jackets. Anyway Choate went on ranting about these four deer, and I told him he had the wrong story and who ever told him that did not get it straight. He insisted that he was right and had heard this from pretty reliable sources. Anyway he left upset that I had shot

four deer. I wish they would get the story right; there were five deer in question not four. Everybody in the country lived off deer or a moose back then, including most Outfitters

Chilco was a person that the past management of the gang Ranch had several run ins with, Wayne always seemed to get along with him though. I remember Wayne asking me to load a quarter or two of beef into his truck, and that he was taking it to Chilco Choate's. Wayne was really making an effort to get along with this guy. Chilco was in fact a valuable asset to have in the mountains; he helped the ranch by telling us where he had seen cattle long after we had left the high country.

Chilco had a Guide Outfitting operation and would take out hunters in the late fall through the backcountry.

He lived on Gaspard Lake, just off Fosberry Meadow with his lovely wife Carroll. Carroll was so pretty with her red hair and such a smart person. I believe she was a nurse. I know it was very nice to be able to talk to a lady so far out in the wilderness.

One day I had invited them to join us cowboys in the cow camp for supper. It was a day that I won't forget. I worked all day cleaning the small log cabin in Fosberry Meadow, and preparing a meal. I remember baking the first and only peach cobbler I have made. I had the wood stove a hoppin. I followed instructions and set it aside to cool. Then I had to take care of some horses and break some ice for the cows. When I returned from that, one of the cowboys had eaten the entire peach cobbler. But the steaks were good and they never complained. It was really nice to see a woman in camp. I had forgotten what they looked like.

Later on, I would find myself working for Chilco in my first guiding job with hunters. It was with one of his Hunters in the spring that I watched old Nero the Grizzly. He walked across the entire meadow in Hungry Valley and all we had was a fishing pole in our hands.

Meanwhile back at the ranch:

I remember the winter of 1965 was very cold. We were told to saddle our best horses, as we were being sent to Summer Range. Every year a winter round up would take place. The ranch had about 150 head of horses out on the mountain over looking Farwell Canyon. It was mid January. We started out towards the old Home Ranch. The snow was getting deeper and deeper as we climbed out of Gaspard Creek and on up into the timber.

When we got to the old Home Ranch, there were three men building log fence. One of them was old Jim Russell. Jim was one of the strongest persons I had ever met. All his life was spent building log fence. I remember that he got real religious. When we arrived, he would join his three young men and they would pray. I told him we needed some prayers if we were to make it to Summer Range before spring.

Once we passed through their camp and glad of it, we were full of religion and headed for Summer Range Cow camp. The going was very tough and slow. The snow was very deep in places and we would try and stick to the timber where it was not so hard. Wayne had put some good hay earlier in the fall in the corrals for this particular winter roundup; it had all been covered and was badly needed when the snowballs flew and the roundup started. No vehicle could make it in to the area in the dead of winter.

When we finally rode over the last ridge we could see the log cabin covered with three feet of snow on the roof. I also saw four large Moose in out hay pile. They had levelled one stack of hay, and were all bedded down in it. I figured we would be here for a long time, so I pulled out a 250/3000 and shot the small one. The meat was great; he had been eating alfalfa for a month or so. When I shot him, he began running up the valley. He went about a half a mile and stood in the trees. I did not want to shoot him again, so I circled him and he went right back to the corrals. He dropped about a hundred yards from the cabin

Walter Hurst and myself

Joe and myself well mounted and all ready to round up Horses.

Then we all got organized and drew a plan as how we were to roundup this area. All the horses had to be driven down to Farwell Canyon it was the only way to go with them. If there were any weak ones, we could bring them to Summer Range with us.

What hay there was left, and the hay the moose had been sleeping in would have to do for all the horses. We saved as much good hay as possible for our saddle horses. They were more important than anything was.

The cabin was freezing cold, the packrats had pulled most of the chinking out of the logs and they were plenty of them. The wind would blow snow right through the logs and into the cabin. In less than one week there were over twenty pack rats hanging on a line outside. There was Joe Auben, Don McDonald a couple of others and myself on the trip.

We started to roundup all the horses that we could find in the pasture, this long ridge was over ten miles in length; it had most of the ranches younger horses, and they could give you a pretty good run for your money but they had been out all winter and were not that fit. So after a few miles they would be a little easier to handle. Our horses were all grain fed and were ready for the job. We had about three head each, and most of them were large horses, good for breaking deep snow. It did not take long before we were moving more and more horse into the corral. It was a big log corral that was great for horses and cattle, but not quite high enough for moose. If a moose could get his nose over the top log, he could jump the corral and push a log over to get to the hay. Soon as the moose saw activity at the cabin, they never came back around.

Before ten days or so, we had about seventy five to a hundred head in the corral. It was into our second week that we heard a plane over the cabin. It was Wayne in a small Super Cub on skis. They did not land, but dropped a note in a can that said to get our butt's over to a certain trail near the breaks of the Chilcotin River.

They had spotted someone driving 8 horses along the breaks towards Big Creek. Who ever it was, was stealing eight head of Gang Ranch horses. The plane did not land because the snow was to deep and went back to the gang Ranch 35 miles away.

We all saddled our best horses and led one spare. Then we cut a trail in the deep snow rotating the lead horse and finally changing onto our spare. In about an hour, we reached his trail that he had made, and with all the horses in front of us we made good time. Our horses were as fit as could be and could stay in a trot all day. When this guy saw us coming up on his trail behind him, he immediately dropped the horses and headed as fast as he could towards the breaks of the Chilicotin River. The ridges were solid snow and ice. Over he went and his horse slid down the side hills like a toboggan. He was on his feet, on his side and flat on his back for several hundred feet. He disappeared and was gone from sight.

Someone had a rifle and quietly got of his horse. He pulled his rifle out, dusted of a large boulder and placed his hat down. Then he took out several shells and patiently waited for him to show at the bottom of the canyon along the Chilcotin River.

He finally showed with his horse badly limping. That's when the shots rang out. One after another, they were getting very close to him. I said you would hit him the next shot if you don't watch it. The answer was, that's what I am trying to do Chris. Luckily for this guy he had a bank to get under and slowly moved up the river. The ranch used to lose many horses and calves this way. It was so vast; we could not cover it all. This bunch of horses was headed for the Chilcotin country, and probably would never have been seem again. I guarantee you that this guy was looking over his shoulder for a while. It would be a while before he set foot on the Gang Ranch again. I know he had the daylights scared out of him that day.

We picked up the young horses. They all had a Gang Ranch brand on them and then we returned down the trail to our horses that we tied up. Then it was on into the corrals at Summer Range. What a day! Our horses, the dogs and us were all pooped and ready for the sack.

The next day Wayne flew in and made the big mistake of landing. There was ample room to land in the vast meadow and fields, what he did not realize was the depth of the snow. Once he was down and landed, there was just too much snow to take off. The Super Cub made several attempts to break a path, but however hard he tried, he just could not get the skis up and on top of the snow with Wayne in the back. Looked like someone was going to have to ride on out with us to the ranch or at least part way. The Super Cub was able to just get airborne without Wayne and left that afternoon.

Come evening when we were all eating supper, Wayne asked me who was the Boss of this outfit. I immediately knew he was up to something. I answered, "Why you are Mr Robinson".Then he said, "I would like to borrow your bedroll". I mumbled softly so he could not hear, "you can kiss my butt Wayne Robinson, you are not getting my bedroll".

He knew I was not going to give up my bedroll, maybe a blanket or two, but not my bedroll. I did not know what down sleeping bags were back then. All I had was a cheap ten-dollar bag with lots of horse blankets thrown on top.

He then brought a bale of hay into the cabin and broke it and covered up with horse blankets and hay. He was ok, it had warmed up, the fire was kept going all night and the temperature was acceptable for January. Besides that, he was an Ex Marine Sergeant.

That morning, when I was putting more wood in the stove, I noticed a large packrat walking along the log by Wayne's head. He had stopped a few feet from where he was. Wayne was half awake and perked up against the bottom log. Guess he was waiting for the coffee to boil and get warm. I ever so slowly reached for this 270-calibre rifle and slowly pointed it in his direction. Then he heard me put a shell in the chamber.

His eyes began to open wide and then I heard this faint cry like he thought I was about to shoot him. He was trying to say something, but it just would not come out. Guess he felt bad about all the things he had done to me, and his life flashed before him. What he didn't realize was that there was a packrat just a foot from his head, and I was about to take care of the matter.

After another little squeal from Wayne, I said, "don't move or say anything Mr Robinson, there is a large rat by your head and I'll get him.

Well you should have seen this huge man come unglued, he jumped up and screamed at me, I took of running in my long johns out into the snow and stood there.

I really was scared to go back in the cabin. He came out on the porch and read me the riot act. He said" I'm going to tell you this only one time you pigeon breasted sob, I never want to come into a camp where you are and find a loaded gun, I mean ever. When I do come to your camp from this day on, I am going to walk right over to the first rifle I see, pick it up and point it at your head then pull the trigger". He said "I know I'll be safe because I know you'll remember everything I say today and you will mind me". Then he let me in the cabin after my feet were turning blue from the cold. All the other guys laughed about that then, and still chuckle about it today.

The next day he had one of my horses saddled and the stirrup leathers lengthened. I new I had lost my saddle. I did not mind that, but I would never give up my bedroll.

We opened the corral gate and cut a trail for the ranch. Thank God Crooked Nose would stop every time I fell off, and that I did many times that day. He was jumping snowdrifts and making sure we did not loose any horses.

I can ride a horse ok without a saddle, but fifteen miles chasing horses was a little hard on the butt. We had about a hundred and twenty five all toll maybe slightly over and for the first five mile it was touch and go with a few. They wanted to go back to their old stomping grounds.

We made it to Ward Creek and spent the night with a logging outfit called Catermol Trethiewy. They had a winter operation and were hauling logs out. From there on I had my saddle returned and a cleared road all the way to the Gang Ranch. The horses travelled right along without any problems. Once they got a few miles away from their old stomping grounds they lined out pretty good. They all had a belly full of good hay that the ranch had delivered to the logging camp. We had about thirty miles to go, and covered that pretty fast.

There were some fine young colts in the herd; luckily we saved a few from being stolen possibly never to be seen again.

This happened every year at the Gang Ranch; horses and cattle would be stolen. Surrounding ranchers would wean the late calves that did not have a brand, and then call the Gang Ranch to come and get their cows that had drifted into their area. They will all deny it, but the truth is many got their start from the gang Ranch.

 I made two trips to Big Creek and picked up eighteen head one winter and over twenty head the next. All the cows had calves weaned at some point from them that fall, and several just a few weeks earlier. This went on all the time, what could you do. All one could really do was to go and get the cows, turn them into the main herd and carry on. It was a small loss in a big outfit and seemed to be accepted.

I remember when a Gang Ranch Cowboy was found shot. His name was Isidore Gillpin. His horse came in to cow camp with his saddle on. They found Isidore at the Corduroy on the way to Sugar Cane jacks. I cannot remember what happened over that, There was a brief investigation and to this day do not know the outcome. Maybe he found some people taking cows out of the country that did not belong to them. Maybe he found a horse thief. Other cowboys said he had a bullet in his head.

Many cattle would not make it out of the mountains. Some would get out into the meadows and get bogged down. Others would eat Milk vetch and larkspur never to see the ranch in the fall.

The Gang Ranch would loose quite a few from the time they were turned out in the summer until they returned in the fall. Years later, I heard there was a big story about the Grizzlies in the high country killing cattle. This I do not believe. We all knew we had to keep the cattle out of the high alpine valleys that had Milk Vetch in them. Those toxic weeds would claim quite a few cows over the summer, bog holes would get a lot, and several cattle were just missed in the mountains.

Come spring the bears had a first course meal all laid out for them. It was left up to them to clean up the dead cows that we unfortunately could not find. I hate to see a bear blamed for something he did not do.

Several horses had over the years been stolen from the ranch and they would sometimes return. They would get loose from the people that took them, and find their way back to their old stomping grounds. We would pick them up from time to time or they would join our horse herd at Cow camp. We could see where these horse thieves had altered the Gang Ranch brand. It did not matter how you looked at the brand, you could always see the JH on the left shoulder. One thing for sure a horse never forgets the place where he was born and raised. They will most always try to make it home, even after a year or two.

I had been at the Ranch four years and Wayne had a 5-year contract to manage the ranch, his term was about to come to an end. When he left, I knew I would be gone shortly after.

The Cowboys that I had worked with would have a long lasting impression on me. Several of the boys I still see once in a while, while others have drifted on. My horses, I do not know what happened to them. I only hope that the next guy had as much pleasure riding them as I did.

I thanked Wayne and his wife for everything and felt kind of sad about them leaving. This man sure did teach me a lot. I did not regret one day of being around him. It was almost five years. There were many more events that one could tell about the Mighty Gang Ranch, enough to fill a book in itself, it was a fine Ranch. They did things the right way while I was there. Good horses and cow dogs are made because there was a lot of work for them. They were used for everything. All the cattle were sorted horseback. Some of the finest working horses that I ever rode came of the Gang Ranch. Guess you could owe that to people like Wayne Robinson, Marvin Guthrie, Loren Wood, Roy Williams, Red Allison and Jack Shearer. They all believed that the best thing for a horse was a wet saddle blanket.

My good friend Loren Wood asked me if I would like to join him and come down to Pendleton Oregon, to see some new country and meet a lot of very good Oregon Horsemen and Cowboys. My face lit up, it was time to move on.

She's downhill and in the shade
CHAPTER TWO
TRIP TO PENDLETON

The car was a dream to sit in, and held all our gear and saddles. My good dog Yeller, one of the best cow dogs to ever come of the Gang Ranch joined us. He had his first experience with a vehicle and new country. It was 1966 that we left.

I had never been to Oregon and it was as pretty as the British Colombia but had much better roads.

Pendleton was mainly a wheat growing area, but had some very good Cattle Ranches in the Blue Mountains and along Butter Creek. There was the Vey Ranch and Cunningham Sheep, which were two of the larger ones. Little did I know that some thirty-seven years later in the spring of 2002, I would be starting twelve head of nice Quarter horses for this ranch.

After getting settled in the town, Loren took me up to the Severe Brothers Saddle shop. They were masters in leather and made the finest saddles that I had ever seen. The trees were bull hide covered and very strong working cowboy saddles. Something you could feel good in and sure not be afraid to rope a large steer or bull. If we would have been riding these saddles when we saw that large Grizzly, we might have stood a chance.

Duff built the saddles and his brother Bill built the trees. The trees were all covered in a Bull Hide that had no cuts or blemishes. These trees were very strong. To this day Severe Bros are putting out quality work. Over the years, this friendship with Duff and the severe family grew to be a major part of my life.

Duff told me that when he got out of the War, he went to work for Hamley's in Pendleton, Oregon. They were the largest Saddle Shop on the West Coast.

I immediately put on order in for one of his saddles, and it was a real masterpiece when Duff and Bill finished it.

Picture of Bill Severe and Duff. After a lifetime of making saddles, this was Duff's last full size saddle that he made. It went to his son Casey.

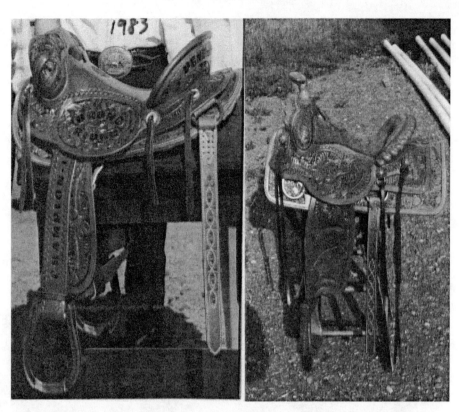

Two fully carved saddles. The left is a Bronc Saddle that a cowboy won at the Pendleton Roundup. The right is a classic and quality hand tooled saddle that they are so famous for.

Some of the most intricate and beautiful hand tooling that went into many of their saddles. The orders would vary from rough out working cowboy saddles; to fully hand carved floral designed saddles

Two Miniature Saddles that went on display at the Smithsonian institute in Washington D.C.

These Decanters are my favourites. They are part of a collection and are some of the most beautiful work that Duff has made. They went on display in the Smithsonian Back in Washington D.C. They are all different with many various Rawhide Knots and carved in leather. There are hundreds of hours in completing this

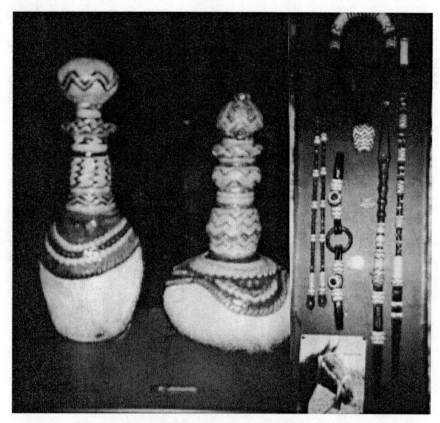

These Decanters on the left were covered from the Scrotums of various Big Game Animals. The fine braiding work of a Bosal is on the right

When I went down to Duffs Corrals, he had horses everywhere, the breeding and quality sure surpassed even the Good horses on the Gang Ranch. They were not the kind you lead and feed, but what I would call, a pretty classy horse that could turn on a dime, slide like a wormed dog, and bounce back like a bad cheque. He had four head that were finished horses. All were so light in the mouth; I was very impressed at the way he worked a colt. I knew Loren had brought me to the right place. I wanted to learn so much from Duff; He sure got so much out of a colt.

Duff was working daily at the saddle shop and in the evenings at his barn where he trained all his horses.

Myself on Graystar in Pendleton Oregon 1966 The horse was owned by Bonnie Guitar, a very good Western Singer and trained by Duff Severe.

One was called Glitter Mount and other was Gay Mount but the one I liked most of all was a grey horse by the name of Graystar. A Singer named Bonnie Guitar owned him. This horse was amazing and could do things, that I never had seen a horse do with all his legwork and lead changes and spins that would unseat most riders.

I liked the groundwork that both Duff and Loren did with their colts; they had patience and were able to obtain a lot of results. Duff was also a real master with a hackamore, and had several that he had braided himself. His rawhide braiding skills were something to look at they still are to this day. A lot of his work went to the Smithsonian Institute for display. He had been honoured with Awards for the Fine Arts. As I write a lot of this book, I look at a showcase full of his work. There is a lot of Rawhide work out there one the market, but there are few Grand Masters. Duff and the Severe Family are that.

He said he had learned some of his knots from a man called Luis Ortega.

Almost all the schooling I incorporate young horses to date, I owe to Duff and Loren they are two fine gentlemen. They have not just started many young colts; they have worked with the finest bred youngsters to real rang tangs that have been running with elk all their lives.

I made friends with a lot of people down there. One man in particular was a ferrier by the name of Lee Ansodequi. Lee was also another good hand with a colt. Besides being the top-notch ferrier in the area.

I heard his wife Barb taught him everything he knows, and believe it. I went out with him on many occasions to help him with some nasty horses. This one day he asked me to join him as he was going to shoe several horses up in the mountains. My job was to hold the horses while he tacked the shoes on. A lady approached us at this one place we went to, she had a mare that was terrible to work with. This mare fought Lee and jerked her leg every few minuets out of his grip. I could see he was getting real tired of this mare and her attitude.

The lady also had two big Rotwieller dogs that were in a large compound. These dogs would hit the page wire fence trying to get to us. They wanted to eat us alive for breakfast. Every time I looked up, the dogs would have their teeth in the wire mesh and hanging on. This lady sauntered over with a tray of Kool Aid, a pitcher and some glasses and asked us if there was anything she could do to alleviate the problems and frustration we were having with her mare.

Lee in the classic style that he is famous for said calmly " Madam if you like I can tell you how to solve all the problems you have here on your ranch. You could take this no count mare of yours and lead her into the pen with those two plumb haywire Rotwiellers pets of yours, those dogs could then kill this horse and eat her right before our very eyes, then after they have done cleaned her up, you could go back in the compound and shoot the dogs. All your problems on your ranch would be solved". She asks us to promptly leave and never come back. As we were packing our stuff I asked lee if this meant that we don't get our glass of Kool-Aid.

Top left picture is Bill Severe's son Randy. He has taken over the saddle shop, and is doing a fine job of continuing the tradition. Right picture is the fine Rawhide work of Duff Severe.

Two other top-notch saddle makers that are part of the Severe Bros Saddle Shop are Bill McCoin and Tim Sweek.

John Groupe and Bill Severe in Northern Canada. John a great outdoorsman who spends all the time he can in the wilderness. He is also a vet in Pendleton Oregon. They joined me in the North one fall.

Duff Severe with his good hackamore horse Exlaxe.

Duff won many reining competitions with this horse over the years.

A bronze was cast of Duff and one of his miniature saddles. It turned out to be the best selling bronze that the sculptor had ever done.

A fine collection of Whiskey Decanters

They are scrotum bags from various wild animals. The necks are all done with beautiful Rawhide Knots. I got most of the scrotums for Duff over the years. These were all on display at the Smithsonian Institute in Washington D.C

She's downhill and in the shade

CHAPTER THREE

The Colts at Empire Valley Ranch

I spent most of the year down in Pendleton and then returned to
Clinton. I was offered a job starting a whole bunch of colts at Empire
Valley. This was a huge ranch that was beside the Gang Ranch on its
Western Border and just down river on the Fraser. The contract I
believe was Don McDonalds and he brought me in on it. Anyway, here
we were at the Empire Valley Ranch owned by the Bryson Family.
Clarence Bryson was the owner and a fine gentleman from the old
school. He really had a beautiful ranch. His sons Mac, Duncan and
daughter Donna along with son in law Don Gillis were a big part of the
ranch and the main ranch hands. Our jobs were simply to get all these
colts going.

  The Blue Bunchgrass was everywhere running the full length of the
Fraser River from the Gang Ranch bridge to McGee flats and Lone
Cabin Creek There were miles of great spring, fall and winter range.
The cattle did well on it, and so did the deer. There were hundreds of
them. They particularly liked a mountain called Clyde Mountain and
Lone Cabin Creek; one could ride up there in the fall and count
upwards of twenty bucks in an hour. I was travelling with Angus
McDonald in Lone Cabin Creek one afternoon. We were in an older
International Scout 4x4 and it was pretty rickety. I pointed to a monster
buck that was about a hundred yards away and had just walked out of
the timber. I asked Angus if he had ever shot a buck. He said no, he had
never shot a deer in his whole life. I handed him the 8mm Mouser that
belonged to Mac.

The buck just stood there while Angus fired shell after shell. I told Angus that this was the largest buck that I had ever seen at Empire Valley or the Gang Ranch, and to take his time. He could not hit the broad side of the barn, so we ran out of shells and went to the main ranch. He said all the way down that the gun was of from all the bumps. We were about two miles from the ranch, when we hit a rut, and the jockey box door flew open. There was one shell lodged in the jockey box. It was the one and only shell remaining out of five.

I immediately turned the rig around, went right back five miles back up to the buck. He had not moved fifty feet. I dropped him in his tracks. I shot the only deer I would ever take on the ranch. It was the largest buck deer of my life. It had a spread of 30+ inches and is still hanging in Mack Bryson's house.

Me with a 30+ inch set of Mule Deer Horns. These horns were taken in the sixty's. They are identical to the buck in Lone cabin Creek.

One fall day, the local Game Warden from Clinton by the name of Jess McCabe arrived. He and I went to McGee flats and counted over 500 deer in an hour. It seemed like the whole flat was moving once we started the drive and the count.

Three large and heavy sets of Mule Deer horns. All taken in the sixty's

There were a lot of deer in the Lone Cabin Creek and Empire Valley Ranch. Just one year later, I would see the biggest slaughter of deer one would ever witness. The Fish and Wildlife would issue up to three tags per person to hunt that area. Hunters were shooting deer everywhere. I watched a hunter shoot a buck, throw a doe off his truck, and load the buck because there was more meat to it. Many occasions one would see Doe's lying close to the road. If you looked around, you would see where another deer had been cleaned.

There was a large bus that arrived from Vancouver with twenty hunters or more hunters in it, It was called BC Safari's. They all shot two to three deer, they had so many on the top of the bus, several would fall of when they were moving down the road to the Gang Ranch bridge.

It was really awful as people were lining up to hunt Empire Valley. It was the end of the mighty deer herd. This reminded me when reading how the buffalo herds were slaughtered.

This has always been a sore spot with me and the Fish and Wildlife; I have nothing against any person taking a deer for food, but to leave carcasses scattered everywhere is a pure waste.

I wonder what Biologist in Victoria figured out the policy and programme for that fiasco. He should have been up there to see the end of an era. What he did not realize was that in the fall, the deer at Empire Valley came from over fifty miles around to be there for the fall rut and to spend the winter on the bunch grass ridges.

All the deer that summered in the Relays, Beaver Valley and as far away as Graveyard Valley would winter at Empire Valley. There were trails a foot deep leading out of the Snow Mountains in the fall. All the tracks on them were deer and they were all headed for Empire valley.

Anyway, back to Empire Valley and the Colts

Well, here we were with a whole pen full of young colts. Some were three-year-olds, some four and five, and a few were a little older. They were big bold and rangy colts.

We were going to do all our work at the corrals in a place called the Gap. It was where the ranch sorted most of the cattle. And believe me, when we took all the horses up there, I knew we had our work cut out for us.

We must have had almost thirty head to do. Don took one and I took one, we went through the herd, and had them separated and in two pens. It worked out pretty good, as we knew whose colts belonged to whom.

It took us all fall and winter to get them started, come spring we had most of them going pretty good. They were not all that bad. I thought they would give us more of problem than what they did. We would ride one, and pack a couple. This went on well into the spring. I always liked to work a colt and also get him used to carrying a pack. One never knows when you will have to pack your horse.

Don was doing pretty well with all the colts except one; I noticed that he kind of avoided him. He was a big bay, much older than all the rest and seemed afraid of nothing. I asked Don if he would like me to give him a hand.

Boy this horse was something, if you even stepped into the pen, and got a little close to him, he would come at you with both front feet flying and meant it.

We got a rope on this guy and another on his front feet. Next came his hind foot that we jacked up, and then we put hobbles on him. We had ropes on everything we could tie down or up, finally a blindfold to boot.

I do not know how old this horse was, but he was no baby and knew what this was all about. I think from what I could see, he had been played with before and whoever did, gave up on him. He was now another year or two older and much stronger.

After all the ropes here and there, we had to work to even get a saddle on him. He fought us from the moment we even looked at him. Just to help him along and not miss out on anything, we hung a set of bleach bottles on his Johnson halter with a couple of pebbles in the bottles.

Then we hung a piece of tarp or canvas onto the saddle. If there were a kitchen sink, we would have probably hung that on. One thing for sure, the time it took to do all this, made it near lunchtime. I have never seen a horse fight a person as much as this guy.

I guess the moment of truce was about to happen, as we eased up and started to untie the assortment of ropes that we had on him. First to come of was the hobbles, then the hind leg was let down.

I made a quick exit up the high logs and to the top log. Don was not far behind me. I had to tell him, the blindfold Don; you have to get the blindfold. After all it was his horse. He eased up to this older colt that was standing motionless and ever so slowly pulled the blindfold down over one eye.

The horse cleared his nostrils with a big snort. That is all it took, and Don started to run for the logs, and the top rail. Don had reached the top rail when this colt made one huge jump, it was so pretty, he brought his hind leg up to the bleach bottles and took them right of his head in one smooth stride and swipe. Talk about an athlete.

Both the halter and bleach bottles came through the air a 100 miles an hour, and caught Don around the neck. He had not turned around on the fence yet and both bottles went whack, like some boxer had hit him. I was laughing so hard; I almost fell of the logs.

Don fell back into the corral and could not see with the Johnson halter and both bottles around his neck.

This colt was bucking like I had never seen a horse buck, he was kicking logs two at a time as he went around. I hollered at Don to get down as he went around. Don could not see a thing, as there was so much dirt in his eyes he just did not know where to turn, but he could hear him coming. Once again he dropped to the ground against the logs. I kind of felt sorry for him, but I sure as hell wasn't getting in there with him. After all, the horse belonged to him. The horse was kicking and debarking the logs as he went round and round. If Don had not been so big and strong, he might have made it under the bottom log and to safe ground but there was only three inches.

I know he tried; he tried very hard to get under that log. Guess he ate to many pancakes for breakfast. The colt finally stopped and Don surfaced, I couldn't help but laugh, to tell the truth, I was laughing so hard, I almost fell of the logs. All I could see were two little white eyes coming from a face that was covered in dirt with clothes to match.

What a horse he was, the next day we did the same thing and that day; he kicked me with both feet with one leg tied up right in the stomach. Don got even that day, as I was squirming on the ground moaning and gasping for air, he was saying ¨˝how do you like that you sob, how do you like that eh"! He kept saying it like a broken record over and over, "how does pain feel"? He was sure getting even for the day before ¨˝.

We did really well with all the colts except this guy. The boss decided we should take him to Dave Perry a stock Contractor at Cache Creek and buck him. Dave Perry gave the horse a name he was called "The Empire", he went on to become one of the top bucking horses in the province for many years. He further threw of the finest cowboys in Canada and the United States. I know when I started to Rodeo, I always drew around him, and glad I did. He flung everyone off, and did it easy.

On day Don and I were taking a team of horses out to a stack yard with a sleigh, we were going to get some loose hay to feed some horses. As we passed this ridge, there was a big four-point buck standing at the top.

Don had his 270 with him in a scabbard slung on the front of the sleigh. He pulled it out and fired one shot. The buck just dropped in his tracks. I held the team while he climbed through six inches of snow up a very steep hill to the buck. It was hard going, but he finally made it. I watched as he dug into his pocket to find his pocketknife and saw him bend over to cut the Bucks throat.

When he stuck the deer, he immediately jumped up and Don stumbled back. Both Don and the deer were glued to each other and both were rolling and stumbling down the hill.

I don't know why I do these things, but I took advantage of the opportunity and fired a shot in the air. I then hollered to Don its ok pard, I'll get him for you, and fired again and again into the air. He didn't know where those shots were going, but I heard him scream "don't shoot you stupid sob, don't shoot." Both Don and the deer were wrapped up with one another. I kept hollering back equally as loud, that I'd get him, just move away and don't worry. I would fire another shot in the air, as they rolled down the hill together. He was real mad at me all day; he actually thought I was shooting at the buck.

That fall, Shots were heard on Clyde Mountain. Some resident hunters had some how got up there and were hunting not just private property, but Mr Bryson's private little sanctuary for the bucks. Clyde Mountain was like a zoo with the huge four pointers we would see up there. We had seen where these hunters had cut the fence and drove up this ridge and into the timber. They covered their tracks up and just disappeared into the bush. Clarence Bryson was determined to find them and kick their butts off the Ranch.

He hired a mane called Baldy Boyd and Baldy came out with his small plane. He circled Clyde Mountain in the early morning, and saw a little trickle of smoke coming from a thick brushy area. He had found them.

The hunters knew they were had, and immediately began dismantling their camp. They had cut brush and put it all around their vehicles to not see them from the air. Baldy said they had bucks strung up everywhere.

The ranch pickup was started and the toughest guys on the ranch were loaded up. There was Don Gillis, Don MacDonald and Dunc Bryson in the truck. I was to be the driver. These guys said they had a plan; it was for me to drive the pickup into their camp while these three tough cowboys were to hide low in the back canopy of the truck.

I was to start some sort of a fight with the hunters over trespassing and shooting deer on private property. They were going to jump out and clean house. What a plan, and I went for it. I had no fear as these guys could really handle themselves in any situation. The bottom line was that they were looking for a good scrap. Kind of like wanting to take the law into their own hands. They were three sheriffs and I was the dumb deputy

The hunters had already dismantled their camp and had about nine big Bucks in the back of their truck. There was horns sticking out and hung everywhere.

What I did not realize was that on the way up to their camp, the latch to open the canopy had locked from the outside. They were holding it slightly open from within with a small block of wood and were all ready to jump out when the time was right. Little did I know that these guys were of no use to me short of smashing everything to break out of the canopy.

I pushed this guy as instructed and planned. He then decked me with one punch; I was down for the count and seeing stars. They jumped in their truck and took of for safety and the Gang Ranch Bridge. Once they crossed it and the Fraser, they were safe. If they could be caught on the Empire Valley Ranch side, it was a different story. The hunters knew this.

Finally Don Gillis kicked either the back door open or the side out of the canopy and they threw me in the back of the pickup and gave chase. It was the wildest ride I have ever been on with some very near misses on the curves going to the Fraser Bridge.

They caught up to the truck, which was flying down the road. They were loosing bucks of the back off their truck, and did not even care. The race was on. Five bucks fell of the truck. Ropes were hanging everywhere, the hunters believe me did not worry about the deer; they were concerned about their lives. Don Gillis and Don McDonald were no people to trifle with and they wanted to kick some ass.

The hunters were very smart, and would not let our truck overtake them. They made it to the Gang Ranch bridge and safety. We chased them for a while and just gave up as we were running out of gas.

I told everybody that night as I put a cold piece of ice on my jaw that I was no longer going to be part of any more "future plans" that they might want to involve me in. There was only one ass kicking that day, and I got it.

That winter, the local outfitter Pete Caldwell stopped into the ranch. The Caldwell family was a pioneer family that had been in the country for quite a while. They were living in Jesmond on the other side of the Fraser River. They had with them some hunters and Charlie Caldwell who was Pete's son. I thought I would play a trick on Charlie. I had asked Charlie if he had seen the new ranch stud that just arrived from Wyoming, I knew he had not, so all the hunters, Charlie and some ranch hands went to the barn to look this stud over.

In the box stall was not a stud, but a huge four point Buck. Eddie Narcise an Indian from Pavilion and I had roped this buck a couple of days earlier from between the stacks of hay. We hog-tied the deer and threw it on the hay sled pulled by a team of horses, took it into the ranch, emptied the horse from the stud's box stall in the barn and turned this large Four Point Buck loose.

We did not realise just how mad the buck was, or the danger involved. When we opened the door to the box stall, Charlie went in and we closed the door behind him. The buck was lying down behind the manger and when he saw Charlie, he was on his feet, the fight was on. We realised then how serious the matter was, but could not do much about it.

Charlie jumped up into the manger with this large rack of horns prodding him in his butt. We pulled him up through the hay shaft into the top of the barn to safety. He had his pants and Jacket torn. Luckily he had on his chaps and thick winter jacket, he could have been barked up pretty good. Anyway the next day, the buck went loose, and we apologised to Charlie. Thirty years later we still chuckle over that one.

Charlie does not think it was too funny though.

Come spring, we were helping the ranch calve out all the heifers and cows we used a lot of the colts working with cattle. The Bryson family had negotiated the sale of the ranch to Mr Bob Maytag from Wyoming; we were there for the transition and continued to work there under new management. Mr Maytag brought in Floyd Felhour as a manager, and everything at the ranch went quite smooth. Floyd was a great person to work for. He always had a smile on his face, and a lovely wife, and family. Bob was an excellent pilot and had a Super Bonanza aircraft that he went back and forth with. It took a pretty good pilot to land at Empire Valley. He did it in the Hayfield just bellow the ranch. His approach was all uphill and tricky to say the least. Bob was a very good pilot.

On one of his return trips from Wyoming, I asked him to stop in Pendleton and pick up my good cow dog "Yeller" that my buddy Duff Severe was babysitting. On their arrival to Pendleton, Duff told Bob and his new wife to never let him off the leash, until he was at the ranch. Anyway, Bob's wife let him go out to relieve himself in Kamloops and yeller went to the mountains and was never seen again. By the time I got there from the ranch, he was long gone. I advertised on the radio and newspaper, but never had any leads. He was a great cow dog and could do the work of three cowboys.

Duke, myself and Yeller in 1966
Two of the finest stock dogs around

It was getting about that time for me to move on, I wanted to go to Kenny McLean's Bronc Riding School and learn to ride Saddle Broncs the proper way. Mr Bryson must have been pleased with our overall work with the colts; he gave us the pick of any horse other than the stud with a 25 brand that was on the ranch. The number 25 was the ranch brand. This was to be a bonus for our good service.

I picked a yearling that was a full brother to the best colt in my bunch.

He was a bay with four white stockings and a nice blaze. I called Loren Wood in Pendleton, and told him to come on up to the ranch and get his horse. I told him that it was a gift from me to him. Duff Severe and Orval McCormach came with him and saw all the work we had done and the colts and went over the ranch pretty well. They were impressed with Empire Valley. They then loaded the young colt up and headed back to Pendleton. I later heard that Loren sold the colt for several thousand dollars. He still owes me a bottle of good whiskey on that one.

69

She's downhill and in the shade

CHAPTER FOUR

THERE WERE BRONCY COLTS AND THERE WERE SADDLE BRONCS

Down I went to the Bonaparte Indian Reservation in Cache Creek it was 1967. Kenny McLean was having a Bronc Riding School at Dave Perry's; Dave was British Colombia's top stock Contractor and had some of the finest Bucking Horses around, along with some very snotty Bulls. There we were some twenty young guys all ready to carve out a place in history as famous bronc riders. What we didn't realise was how many times we would get bucked off, before we decided to stay up there on their backs. It did not take us long to start pulling our heads out of the ground. Malcolm Jones was putting on a Bareback Riding

School following this Saddle Bronc School. The next week was quite a learning experience and sure taught a person how to find timing and balance with a bucking horse. The moment we goy out of time with him, we were on the ground. There was a lot more to it than that, but Kenny was a fine instructor and was a World Champion Cowboy at that. He had patience, a big smile, was always there to help you out on your bucking horse if you asked him. Kenny had a Grey horse that was one of the best calf Roping horses on the circuit. I believe he was Music Mount Bred.

Kenny on WarPaint at the Ellensburg Rodeo. Kenny helped more cowboys than anyone get started in Rodeo. He was an excellent instructor

It was there that I made friends with one of the best cowboys I have ever met. He was Archie Williams a local Indian from the Bonaparte Reserve. He was the man that picked you up off the Saddle Broncs, if you made it that far. I spent one whole winter with Archie and his lovely wife "Bugs". Archie's father was called "old Dad" and was a fine gentleman.

This man was a great hand with a horse, he could get in there right beside a bucking horse and save your bacon. Whenever I got in a bind and prayed for help, Archie was there to bale me out. He rode a horse called Joker and another called John, they were Dave Perry's top Pickup Horses. I would later get to pickup at several Rodeos for Dave, and ride John.

This one Rodeo at Lillooet, A bull was turned loose in the arena covered with ten and twenty dollar bills. It was intermission time and there was a half hour break. Whoever was brave enough to go in and get the money had a chance to become instantly rich.

There were some fifty hippies who jumped in to collect. The bull made one swipe through them, wiped out about twenty and jumped the fence. This bull took one look at fifty hippies, and said, I'm gone. Archie looked at me, and I looked at him, we both had smiles on our face. Out the gate we went to bring back the bull. Just outside the rodeo grounds in a field, we head and heeled the bull and within moments the manager of the Rodeo came flying down the road in a pickup asking us if we had taken any money off the bull. I replied, what money, the hippies got it all.

Archie Williams and Myself bringing the Bull back. Please note all the money still glued to his back

We had fine bucking horses to learn on. Many were quite nice and some easy to ride, then there were the ones that you sure wanted a deep seat, and prayed for the best.

National Final Horses such as Black Hawk, Deuces Wild, Big Enough, Witch Doctor, Paper Doll, Bo Jangles, Caribooster, Fox, The Empire and many others were in his string. One year, I went with Dave and a load to Omak, all horses were joining a truck going to the National Finals in Oklahoma. Thirteen Horses went there from his string; only one horse was rode that was "´Big Enough". ´ They won the go-round that day on him.

Dave was thrilled that his horses had done so well. Time after time, they flung the best cowboys in the world off. Dave Perry loved his bucking horses. He would often call them as he sat on his pickup horse. When the cute gate opened the horse would swap ends and turn on a dime when they heard his voice. Usually the cowboy was picking himself out of the dirt about then. All that would happen of course if Dave did not like you.

Myself picking up on that good horse "John" at the Clinton Rodeo

Right after the school we hit the road, all heading out to make our fortune. I went to Alberta and spent the whole summer over there working all the Vold and Kessler Rodeos. They spanned across Alberta from north to south and then to Manitoba. I did not ride very many horses at the Rodeos that year, it was my first year, and the stock was the best in Alberta. There were some great Saddle Broncs around, and any one of them could put you in first place and win the rodeo. My problem was that I just did not have the experience. Every Rodeo I went to, there were five of six World Champions in the chutes next to me. It felt kind of intimidating. But that's life and the show goes on.

Horses like Powder River, Bugle boy, Bar Seven X, Hat rack Trails, Rodeo News and many more. One thing for sure, when one started to ride these horses, you were riding the best that Canada had to offer and that was my goal.

Things were not going that well for me in the arena, these horses were flinging me off day after day and I was not making any money at it, matter of fact I was starving to death. I was catching rides and travelling with two great cowboys they were John Dodd's and Dale Trottier. I did not know how long they were going to keep feeding me and putting up with this.

I met a man that saved my life and offered me a job while going to all the Rodeos. It was Jon Temple from Cleburne Texas. Jon was the Clown and Bullfighter for Wayne Vold that year. He could see I needed a good square meal, and asked me if I would consider working his barrel when the bulls came out

. This meant I would have to be out there when the Bull Riding began, and then would have to assist him in fighting a bull or two. What the hell, I jumped at the chance and said, "I'm your man". Jon then told me he would pay me $75 per performance. I could not believe what I was hearing and could not wait to get all dolled up in the clown clothes that they wore. Jon had a very good Clown Act and was an excellent Bullfighter.

He was as caddy on his feet as a cougar and could play games with the bulls, even the very mean ones.

Myself, Jon Temple, Woody and Jay Sissler at my debut in fighting bulls. 1967 in Wainwright, Alberta, Canada.

The Premier Performance was a town called Wainright, Alberta. I was to start my career as a clown and bullfighter at Wainright. Wayne Vold had several good Bulls that would sure hunt you. I had watched them pretty close and figured everything would be fine. I even had visions of becoming quite wealthy at this, and already was figuring out how I was going to spend all this money that I was to earn fighting bulls. What it really meant was that I could graduate from hot dogs to a hamburgers.

Anyway the Bulls came out and for the first three or four it was piece of cake. Jon helped the cowboys of the bulls and then he said we have to watch closely for the next bull. His name was V7 and had a white face, with long sweeping horns. V7 came out, and bucked his rider off. He went up to the end of the arena where all the calf ropers hang out and set his sights on me. I to this day do not know why he did not choose Jon; he was closer, and trying to get his attention. V7 wanted me and he began to come at me. He picked up speed and I figured I could out run him to the Barrel.

We also had a dummy hung up on a cable that we could move in front of the bucking cutes when we wanted to. I got scared and went for the dummy instead of the Barrel. This was a very big mistake. When I jumped up to grab the cable and put my legs on the dummy's shoulders, my weight brought it right down almost touching the ground.

Here I was with V7 full steam ahead with those huge sweeping horns and coming right for me. It was like a scene with the fox and the roadrunner, there was nothing I could do. V7 hit me so hard, he threw the dummy and me right up in the air, the announcer Bob Chambers was right parallel with me, and he was pretty high up in the announcer's booth. Luckily when I came down, V7 had gone right into the catch pen gate. I was out cold and out of wind for a several minuets. The crowd went wild and thought it was a great act. The cowboys packed me of to the cutes. Jon ran up to see how I was, and said "Hurry up and catch your wind. We have a couple of good fighting bulls next in the chute and ready to go".

The only words that I could utter when I got my wind was," I think I just quit, I quit this job. And you don't even have to pay me for this performance". Jon did pay me though, but it was the first and only time I fought bulls at a Rodeo. The crowd thought this was all part of a good act.

Glenn Randall from Newhall California.

Glen was on tour with all his trick horses and was working all the rodeos for Vold Rodeo that year. I was offered a job as his assistant and gladly accepted, because it sure was a turning point in my life with horses.

Glen Randall was, and is to date the finest Horseman; I have ever had the privilege of knowing. He had a great Circus act that he put on with seven Palomino horses, he also had on board a Black Horse called Vic that did all the stunts for Fury in the Hollywood movies.

Glen had supplied horses to the movie industry for years, and his horses performed in all the major films. Even the big chariot race in the classic film Ben Hur was part of his career that spanned a lifetime with the industry. What impressed me the most was his ability to get the most advanced movements in High Level Dressage with absolute ease and lightness in hand with this one Buckskin horse. He was not even a Warm blood or one of those European Breeds that they use for dressage. On centre stage in Calgary at the night show, he brought the house down with all the most difficult, beautiful and precision movements one could do with a horse.

When they performed, it was as one, the horse did movements, such as a Passage on Two tracks and the grand finale was a Canter Backwards. This movement took the highest level of collection with the horse finally cantering on the spot, then, he leaned backwards slightly, shifted his weight and the horse cantered backwards for several steps. This horse had to have very strong hocks to be able to do this, as all his weight was on his hocks. He made it look so easy. Several movements were things you would see in a Circus, while others were very difficult high school movements. I learned from Glenn all about obtaining and maintaining the direct flexion at the Poll, and not the withers, allowing a horse to balance himself.

A person could write several chapters on Glenn Randall's horsemanship skills. He was the Grand Master and is to date a person that should go down in history as one of the finest of the century. There have been a few books written about several European horsemen that stand out as the finest. Glenn was equally as good if not better and deserves a place in history.

I worked for Glenn that summer and rode broncs at every Rodeo Vold and Kessler had. At the end of the season everyone was preparing to go south. Glenn had taught me a lot. He asked me to join him and go and work with him on movie sets. He said that he could hire me fulltime and remain on tour.

I said goodbye to a fine man and wished our trails would have crossed again down the road. Unfortunately they never did.

 I had the call of the mountains that was just around the corner. Fall was here and it was time to start preparing for Hungry Valley, Lost valley, the Snow Mountains and Guiding Hunters.

She's downhill and in the shade

CHAPTER FIVE

CHILCO AND GASPARD LAKE

This was my first year working for Chilco Choate as a guide. I knew almost every inch of the Gang Ranch, and he paid a good wage for those days.

The moose were plentiful, and there were a lot of Big Bucks in Churn Creek and his area to guide in. I worked with an Indian who was a very good Moose hunter; his name was Jimmy Seymour from Canoe Creek Indian Band. This guy I believe could smell a moose and had eyes like a hawk.

One Day I was at the main Camp in Gaspard Lake. I saw Chilco coming across the Meadow leading a packhorse and had one tailed to him, that tailed horse was ´´Willybill´´, my favourite packhorse. I had walked out to open the pole gate to let him in with his horses. They had just moved my camp from Churn Creek back to main camp.

He got of his horse and let the reins and lead rope drop about fifty feet from the gate. He came over to help me with the poles. He was wearing a big pair of batwing chaps and made a heck of a noise when he moved around. Then he returned to his horse and reached for the reins. The other two packhorses that were head and tailed had walked a short distance wanting to get into the Corral and get the packs of.

When Chilco walked towards them, they spooked from the noise of his chaps and walked a little farther away. He must have had a bad day, because the next thing I saw was unbelievable, he pulled out his rifle from his scabbard on his saddle horse, and fired a shot right in front of the first packhorse. I guess he thought they would stop in their tracks. What they did, were hit a trot and began moving up the trail, which they had just come down. The next shot, they were in a gallop. The first horse leading the second, it was something I had never seen before, and could not believe my eyes.

I heard the pack boxes breaking half a mile away on the trees, they were like rifle shots going of as the wooden boxes and saddles broke. Chilco said that he would track them the next day and pick up what was left. The sad part about this spectacle is that Willy Bill my favourite packhorse and the other horse have never been found to this day. One doesn't even read stories like what I just witnessed in a Zane Grey or Louis Lamoure Western Novel.

There was another episode that fall that really irritated me and felt utterly disgusted with what I saw.

There was a ranch down at the end of the valley called the Sky Ranch. They apparently had a stud horse that would occasionally roam up into the Gang Ranch area with a few mares Several times I ran across him up in what they called The Wales Place and Wild Tee meadow. One day, I was riding down from Hungry valley to Chilco's main camp with a hunter and we heard some thrashing around in the bush, there was a lot of noise, and the horses we were riding had their ears pricked forward and moved cautiously through the bush.

There in front of us was the Sky Ranch stud with several arrows in him. I could not believe what I was looking at, and proceeded to put him out of his misery. He was breathing his last when we arrived and heard us coming down the trail. I was furious, I could not prove anything, but there was only one person in camp that had a bow. They knew I was very upset and he left shortly afterwards. From that day forth, I lost what respect I might have had for this guy and several others.

If the Sky ranch had known what happened that day to their Stud Horse, there would have been some heads rolling at Gaspard Lake.

The day after this happened; I left for Hungry Valley and beyond. I had several fine hunters with me that fall; one was Gail Roberts from

Eugene Oregon. Gail was a contractor and loved to hunt the big Muley Bucks. I took Gail and another person who was an accountant up into the Relays, that was as far as we could go in the hunting area, and was the finest deer country that I knew of. Gail got a huge deer up there and

It weighed so much that it had to be quartered. We just could not lift it onto the packhorse. We finally settled for two packhorses and halved the deer. He was as large as a yearling moose, and is the heaviest deer I have hunted to date. The other hunter got a very large buck in the Beaver Mountains over the hill from Relay. We were sleeping in a small three-man tent, and had the deer all hung up in a tree for the night. All the horses were staked and hobbled and one had a bell on.

The next morning, there was one inch of fresh snow hat had settled overnight. When we opened the tent flap in the morning, there were two very large Grizzly tracks less than two feet from our tent door. A pretty good sized grizzly had checked out all our camp in the night, pulled the deer down from the tree, and drug it some 200 yards into the bush and began eating it.

What upset me more than that was the horses had let me down as watchdogs.

They always let me know when something was wrong and a bear was around or near camp. This bear slipped in right under their noses.

I told the hunters that we could have a grizzly the next night, we could stay up and get him, and I knew he would be back for his deer. The accountant said that we were getting out of there as soon as daylight came. I guess he did not like the thought of six hundred pounds of grizzly that close to his head.

I continued working there that fall, and returned for a Spring Bear hunt in Hungry Valley in May.

That was the year we saw Nero the Grizzly. He was huge, and as big as any Gang Ranch Angus Bull. Nero was as black as the ace of spades, and weighed in well over 1200 lbs.

There were a lot of grizzlies in the valley; we estimated at least 8 bears were travelling up and down from the different tracks in the snow. It was mid day, around May 25th and we were going down to Fish Lake at the bottom end of Hungry Valley, the main valley was open, but there still was a lot of snow in the timber. When old Nero came out of the trees on the other side of the valley. I knew it was him from his size and colour.

There was nothing we could do, but watch as he moved right across in front of us without a care in the world. It was as if he owned the valley and nothing scared him. My hunter regretted not taking his rifle along with his fishing pole. After he passed us, we went over and measured his track in the snow and mud; it was 16 inches on his back pad

There were hunters that had hunted this bear for many years, I had seen his tracks often over a five year span, from Relay Creek to Hungry Valley, the closest I had ever come to him in the past was when we took the 100 horses up to relay that one summer. I was in the lead, and his tracks were right in front of me crossing the creeks. Now here he was after all those years. The bear was latter shot on the other side of Big Creek I was told, he weighed about 1400 lbs. and is well up in the Boone and Crockett book on the trophy heads of the world. His skull measurements were logged in at one eighth of an inch under twenty-seven inches. The closest we came to a grizzly that spring was seeing old Nero.

The next Hunter was Neil Esterla from Springfield, Oregon. What a neat guy he was; I spent a most enjoyable ten days with him and connected with a large buck in the Big Basin. This buck saw me when I rode over a hill and onto a trail. He was about one hundred yards away and stood up under a tree. There were limbs all around him. I told Neil to get of his horse quickly, and shoot that deer. He jumped off and

Neil at Trappers Camp in Wild Tea Meadows

Neil Esterla and I on Relay Mountain, The Gang Ranch

Glassed him first. Then he turned to me and said' Chris this deer is a doe'. I told him to just shoot the deer and don't even talk about it, just shoot. He did, and when he dropped it seemed like half the tree came down with him. His horns were magnificent, and I guess he couldn't see any horns for the branches and limbs. That was the second largest buck that I had ever seen. The first was in Lone Cabin Creek.

One night while Neil and I were in the lost valley camp, I picked up a book. It was just by chance that I reached for it from a pile of books. There before me was a letter my boss Chilco Choate had written about seeing a having an encounter with a Sasquatch. The whole book was about Sasquatch sightings throughout the Province and Washington, his was one of the best letters in the whole book

I could not believe what I was reading, and after digesting all the crap that I could stand, I spoke up. I said that I was reading a very interesting chapter on Sasquatches, and that the best story was yours Chilco. I started to drill him on this letter, and he stopped doing the dishes and there was a lot of silence. Then, I asked where this all took place and all these boulders that this Sasquatch was supposed to have been in, their location etc etc according to this story. I had ridden up this valley in question, and never ran across any boulders. There was a lot of stuttering and silence, and then I asked who the hunter was that he had with him, he replied that the hunter had since died. Ya, I bet he died of shock from seeing a Sasquatch. I rode this area for seven years both for the Gang Ranch, and working for Chilco, and the closet track that I could come to anything was that of old Nero or a Grizzly.

When my boss starts to see Sasquatch, and write stories about it, it's time to saddle a fast horse and move on. That's exactly what I did and have never been back.

CHAPTER SIX

MY BEST YEAR IN RODEO

1968 was here, and once again the Rodeo season had started. This proved to be my best year and I made more money this year than expected. Not only was I happy about that, but also I got to meet and get to know some of the finest Bronc Riders and Rodeo Cowboys in the business. There was Trapper and John Dodds, Ramjet, Winston Bruce, Allan Thorpe, Peter Newberry, Phil Doan and so many more; that one could write several chapters. I still remember some of the famous rides they made. Rides like Myrtis Dighteman when he rode Volds V40 at Ponoka, and the Judge said he slapped the bull, one week later, he rode Head-hunter at Williams Lake, and once again, the Judge said he slapped the Bull. The finest Bareback ride I saw was Joe Alexander on the great mare Necklace at Ponoka. (Incidentally, that mare had a Gang Ranch brand on her left shoulder). Peter Newberry made one hell of a ride on that great bucking horse Bo Jangles at the Kamloops Indoor Rodeo. There was the Great Malcolm Jones, Ted Vayro, Mel Hyland, Kenny McLean, Ivan Daines, Tom Bews, Pat McHugh, Jimmy Dix and Denton Moffat and my hero, the immortal Saddle Bronc rider Marty Wood.

Marty was like an old steam engine that would not stop running. After all his competitors quite riding. Marty was still going strong.

Marty was asked one day by a younger cowboy, if he would come over and help him set his binds on his bronc saddle, the kid said, they just did not feel right. Marty replied, " Binds, binds, binds that's all I hear from you guys is binds. If you want more binds, go and eat some cheese". Then he said, "If you were a real bronc rider, you should be able to ride bucking horses in an apple box".

Many years later after he finally quite riding, I visited him out side of Pendleton, Oregon. He asked me if I would like one of his many buckles that he had won over the years. Marty had won the World Championship three times and the Canadian Championship several times also. I dug in this suitcase and pulled out several of the most prestigious buckles in the sport of Rodeo. I put on the World Championship buckle and turned to my good friend Peter Newberry and jokingly said, " what do you think Peter, do you think it looks to gaudy on me"?

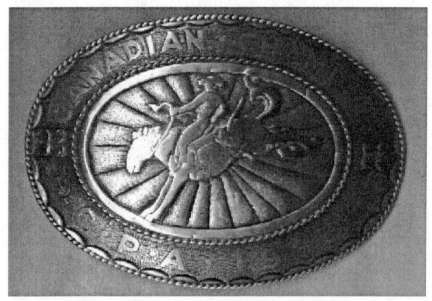

The 1963 Canadian Championship Buckle that Marty gave me.

I could not bring myself to accept or wear the World Championship Buckle. I humbled myself and settled for the 1963 Canadian Championship Saddle bronc buckle and wear it most every day.

I then asked Marty why he let Winston Bruce and Kenny McLean win the World Championship right out from under his grasp by just a few dollars back in the sixty's. He replied in his usual style "because I liked them." Marty still works with horses and has made some great winners with Thoroughbreds

The young champion, pictured again at age 40, and displaying his classic, swashbuckling style at Cheyenne's Frontier Days where he won the average for the first time this past summer.

The Greatest Saddle Bronc Rider of all time. The immortal Marty Wood from Bowness, Alberta. Here is the style that won him Three World Championships

Top picture

Peter Newberry at Williams Lake Stampede on the great Dave Perry Bareback Bucking horse 'FOX'. Peter had the stuff Champions are made of.

It was a real privilege to Rodeo with these guys and get to know them. They rode some of the toughest stock thrown at them by Vold and Kessler Rodeo Contractors, and did it with a smile. I got to see the famous Ellie Louis ride at Calgary and the two all time great Bucking Horses Misty Mix and Big John do their stuff.

That year, I got to draw and ride some great bucking horses myself. Colonel Blue, Suntan, Bar Seven X, Whiz Bang, Hat Rack, Bugle Boy, Powder River, Big Enough and A few that I sure did not like to mention like El Rancho of Kessler's. During the summer between

Rodeos, I went to help Malcolm Jones in Alberta. One day, I was along side of a fence tightening the wires and fixing the slack in the fence. I had a horse loaded down with fencing tools, wire and a few steel posts lashed to the saddle. These cowboys had driven up the road with a trailer to get Malcolm's top Bulldogging horse to take to a rodeo. He had the best horse in the sport of rodeo, and all the top cowboys liked to use him. Many thousands of dollars was won on that horse every year.

Anyway, they asked for directions to collect the horse at the ranch. I told them if they were not in such a big hurry and waited just a few minutes, I would unsaddle him and they could load him up right there. The horse they were looking for was carrying all my wire, posts and nail bucket.

I thought they were going to die; they said nobody move don't even move a muscle, they were very serious and meant it. They proceeded to unsaddle him, load him, and took of down the road shaking their heads. What the hell a little fencing never hurt a champion. Matter of fact, he liked the work.

Malcolm 'Rip' Jones with that great Bulldogging Horse." Rip" won the Canadian Championship in several events several times over. He was par excellent one of the finest bareback riders of all time.

I went to several Rodeos with Malcolm and then teamed up for a while with his brother Allan and Gordon Vayro. We all worked a few Rodeos together in Montana before returning to British Colombia.

WINSTON BRUCE ON 29 BIG JOHN (KNIGHT) SAN ANTONIO '66

One of the greatest Bronc Riders of all time was Winston Bruce from Alberta, Canada. Here he is in his true classic form on that super Bucking Horse Big John

*The Great Canadian Saddle Bronc Rider Ivan Daines from Alberta
on a National Finals Horse*

*Mel Hyland winning Pendleton and who won the World
Championship twice. Showing classic style on Volds famous
Canadian bucking horse "Swanny" This horse was one of Volds top
Bucking horses for many years.*

Not only was Wayne Vold Alberta's top Stock Contractor, He was one of the finest Bronc Riders to come out of Canada. Here he is showing Classic form and real style on a saddle Bronc. Wayne put together a fine string of bucking horses, and looked after them well.

*Doug Flannigan on a tough horse to ride. Doug was on of the very
best Bareback Bronc Riders to come out of Australia.*

I then met one of the nicest persons in the Sport Of Rodeo. Her name
was Geraldine McLaughlin. Geraldine was travelling with her mother,
and was doing her best to win the Canadian Championship in the Barrel
Racing event. She was so good and had her horse working like a dream.
He did not look like he was ever going that fast around the barrels, but
there were no unnecessary or wasted moves. They both were serious
contenders for the Championship.

I travelled some with them, and went and helped their father out on the
ranch in Pincher Creek Alberta in between rodeos. He had a beautiful
ranch nestled up in the Rocky Mountains outside of Pincher Creek
Alberta. His name was Judge McLaughlin and a fine hard working
gentleman.

Geraldine was a very good horsewoman and had a nice way with her horse. I never saw her yanking and jerking on her horse, she had nice hands, handled him right and he ran well for her.

That year she won the Canadian Championship and I was sure proud of her. She worked hard for it and deserved every Nickel she won. Geraldine had a sister called Julie. One day when we returned from a rodeo, Julie asked me to come down to the barn and see her new barrel prospect.

I went down and low and behold was a horse that I used to gallop at the track a year or two ago His name was Gringo Boss, his sire was Pit Boss and he had a world of speed. When she asked me what I thought of the horse, I rattled of his name, his track history and a few major problems that he had with his legs. She was amazed that after all the places for 'Gringo Boss' to go, he would wind up in Pincher Creek, Alberta. She trained the horse and got him to turn the barrels quite well, it was a question if his legs would hold out. She cracked him out at the Calgary stampede and believe she won a third or split a third on him. I did not see Gringo Boss after that. I do not believe he was sound enough to make it on the Rodeo Circuit

I placed in thirteen rodeos that year and got to ride six or seven different horses that had won at one time the bucking Horse of the Year award. It was a good year for me, I never got hurt that year, and I felt great about going to the mountains and getting ready for Fall Hunting. I was a happy camper.

94

Me on a horse at Calgary in 1968

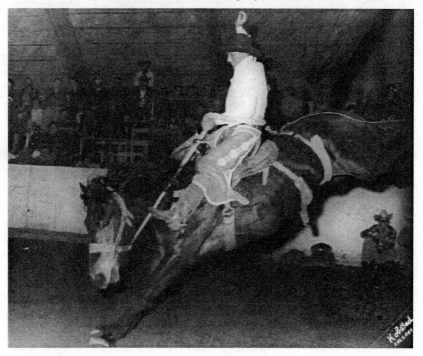

Me on another horse at Stavley Indoor Rodeo in Alberta in 1968 🖐

Dale "Trapper"Trottier showing the determination in riding a tough horse. Dale won the Canadian Championship several times over. I saw this ride at Calgary and it was unbelievable.

My other hero and The Greatest Bull Rider of all time. John "Spook" Dodds from Ponoka, Alberta. Not only was he the finest Bull Rider, He was the smoothest Pool Shark in town. I think I bought John more meals over a game of Pool than anyone. John now is very active in the Movie Industry.

Malcolm "RIP" Jones not only was he a Great Bareback Bronc Rider; he was a real gentleman and a good guy to work for.

The tough Canadian Champion Allan Thorpe in true style. Taken at a Rodeo In Canada.

Five time World Champion The legend himself Joe Alexander.

One of my all time favourite cowboys from South Of the Border

1977 World Champion Bronc Rider J.C. Bonine 🤚

She's downhill and in the shade

CHAPTER SEVEN
GARY POWELLS OUTFITTING

Fall was rolling around, and it was time to get ready to start hunting again it was my very last rodeo of the year, a good and dear friend of mine by the name of Cheryl Callison had introduced me to an Outfitter Called Gary Powell. Cheryl was raised in the North and was the daughter of Lynch Callison a well known Outfitter and guide. She is my life long buddy and still is to day.

This was the start of a fourteen-year working relationship with Gary Powell. Every fall I would head up to his area for the finest hunting outside of Banff and Yellowstone National Park. I would take about five to six Stone Sheep Hunters out. They would have tags for Sheep, Goat, Elk, Moose and Caribou and occasionally a Grizzly tag. Everybody filled their tags. Every season there would be three or four Rams over 40 inches come in. Gary himself came in with a 46 incher that he got of Samuel's Mountain, I helped cape it at base camp. He was guiding a guy who had shot a large 40 + incher when the larger ram showed himself. They did not even know he was there, so Gary took him and deserved it. To get a Ram of Samuel's was quite hard, as there was a lot of brush; not you're typical type of sheep hunting.

 The Muskwa and Gathto were the two main rivers in the area on the Northern side; there was the Tuchodi on the other. This country held a large and healthy elk population. We would see upwards of ten six pointers every day and it was for many years like a zoo, there was so much wildlife.

A lot of this was to do with excellent management on the part of Gary with some good burns to have good winter forage for the game. At that time the Game department frowned on burns. Now, I see they practise this in a lot of areas throughout the province.

The very first day on the job, he asked me to go to a shed and take some salt up for the horses; this shed was about a half a mile from the lodge. When I arrived at the salt shed there were also 14 head of 6-point Elk staring at me, all in the velvet and not the slightest bit worried. Gary had made a no shooting area around the main lodge for a couple of mile radius. Everything in there was safe, and all these six pointers knew it. Those rules applied all the years I was there, and everyone respected them.

I guided some very interesting people over the seasons at Gary's; I got some very nice Stone Rams and the Elk hunting was bar none the best.

I was sure impressed with the way he ran the Outfit, his wife Olive was a super cook and knew more recipes on good cooking and how to prepare venison than anyone. This was all passed down to her two daughters Connie and Rhee.

The horse herd consisted of several hundred good horses. They were all raised in the hunting area. I had a horse called Roger that remained with me his whole life and was one Good Mountain horse he bailed me out of many a jam.

He amazed me when he could come home in the dead of night in a snowstorm. You could not see five feet in front of you. I would swear we were heading in the opposite direction and then all of a sudden, there was our camp. I just learned to rely on him a lot in those situations, he never failed me.

Gary was also a Bush Pilot. He could do things with a Super Cub that made him one of the best I have ever flown with. He would supply the smaller camps once they left Main Camp. A very nice Lodge was at main camp, also the hangers and good runway for the aircraft.

My first hunt was up in Powell Creek. We had two hunters from the US and all the packhorses were ready to go. We started up the Gathto

River, crossed it several miles up, and headed up Jack Creek, over the pass into Powell Creek and on into camp. She was a pretty good camp considering the elevation. Not bad horse feed; firewood was good, as we always had to keep the cook happy. The cook was Gary's daughter Rhee and her brother Grant was the other Guide.

Hy Erickson, Jerry Campbell, Mickey Simpson and Rhee

She could make a tent camp so comfortable even in the middle of a snowstorm.

Packing in to Powell Creek

As we started up Jack Creek coming in, we saw 5 very good Rams on the left and were thinking about going after them. We had all the horses and camp ahead, so we left them for another day and went on over the mountain to Powel Creek and set up camp.

Just above us at camp was a very sheer cliff and mountain. Every day, at a certain time a monster Billy Goat would come out to the edge and lay down with his front feet hanging over the cliff wall.

This Goat had quite a reputation, as every Sheep Guide had made a try for him including the boss, and he was still there.

I thought I would be on his list too. But that would come after I secured the clients Ram. That came the second day out of camp. Just up at the head of Powel Creek were three nice Rams. One had a nice full curl and the others were slightly smaller. We moved into position and they came out in front of us. The three Rams did not even know we were there. The big feller dropped, and there was my first guided Stone Ram. He measured at 36 inches on both horns.

Now for that big Billy Goat. The next day we did not need any horses, as we were going to do some major climbing right from camp. Here I am doing the same thing everyone else had tried.

We had scanned the face, and figured out the best way up. After five hours of solid climbing, we were near the top and I have never been so scared in my life. There was no place to put your feet, and the face was a 500-foot drop straight down to camp. I made it across the face, and had about a twenty foot section and we were home free. Those twenty feet were the longest in my whole life. I was shaking like a leaf and with the help of my hunter, who was an Ex Special Forces and climbing expert, made it to Terra Firma. Only twice in my life, I have ever said my prayers, this was the first, I actually thought I was a goner. We thought we had the wind in our favour, it was swirling around up there, and you did not know which way it was blowing. We were determined that we would have him by afternoon, we moved into position and he was not there. You could smell him everywhere and there were pieces of his long white hair all along the rocks. I eased out as far as I dared to his bed that he used, and saw, it was very deep and had been well used.

That was the end of him; we were running out of time and needed to get back down the mountain. This time, we took an easier route, which was straight down through a waterfall. It was the only way out other than that wall. You could not have got me across that wall for a Million Dollars or the World Record Goat. He could remain on his mountain and die of old age for all I cared. There were a lot easier Goats to get than him.

When we got back to camp, he was hanging his legs over his bed looking down at us chewing his cud. I saw the Goat many times and this Billy had more spotting scopes on him than any other animal. He towered over all the other full-grown adults and had enormous horns that were world record class. I watched the Billy for many years, every time I went to Powel Creek; he was there to meet us. Every time we left Powel Creek, he was there to say goodbye. Until one year he never showed. Guess he did not make it through the winter and died of old age. I do know, that if anyone could have got him, they would have had a near World Record.

I asked the hunter to take a five hundred yard shot on this ram. A storm was coming in, and turned out to be the last ram of the year

We only took one hunt a year out of that valley. It was always good to me, and I always got a dandy Ram for my hunter. Grant got a nice Ram for his hunter and we moved out to Goat Camp a few days ride away.

That first year into Powel Creek, one of the packhorses fell off a cliff, and wound up down in a hole that he could not get out of. I felt sorry for the horse; he was a young one and probably his first trip into the mountains. Anyway, we had to take his pack off, re pack a saddle horse and move on. Grant put the horse down, now we were short one horse. I walked from Powel Creek to Blue Lake, which was the next camp over a mountain range and up a nice valley through a large burn. When we arrived at Blue Lake, it was Magnificent. The surrounding mountains were rugged and the lake was full of Dolly Varden and Grayling. There was lots of horse feed and the weather was Co-operating. The game rolled in, and the hunters were happy all tags had been filled.

 Blue Lake

Cam with grouse on his first sheep hunt with me in Granny Creek

It was at Blue Lake that some Resident Hunters had shot a large Bull Moose in the Lake. They cut the Horns of and left the carcass to drift from one side to the other. This was very dangerous for any floatplane landing. If they ever hit a pontoon with the moose, it would crash for sure. I went out in a small boat with somebody and hooked a rope around a leg and we towed him to shore. We left him tied up to a tree on the shore.

It was not very many days later that Garry and I were flying with the Super Cub over Blue Lake. We saw a black line through the soft meadow. A Grizzly had drug the whole moose out of the lake and buried it. Things like that amazed me with the strength of a bear. Here a grizzly drug a whole 1600 lb carcass out of a lake and up into the bush.

There were several of the finest sheep guides in the north working there. Besides Grant, there was Doug Wiebe who I got to spend many years working with. There was Carl Vig and Duane Powell; both excellent guides who knew every inch of the area.

 These guys were the backbone to the Sheep camps. It was always a competition who was going to get the big daddy that fall. Then there were the lower camps that catered to the elk hunters. There was Braden Powell and Dennis Gunn who were the best Elk and Grizzly guides in the camp. These men were all very professional and knew their jobs well. They could throw a diamond hitch so fast; the horse did not know he was being saddled. They had to, because when the hunts were leaving main camp, several would go out at once. This meant some 80 head of horses would be packed or saddled in no time at all. The farthest camp would go first and if a horse acted up, he got one of the heavier loads.

Packing out the last hunt of the year. Time to head south
The weather can change from summer to winter overnight.

Two nice rams at Blue Lake
Hunter on the left, I forgot his name. It's me on the right.

Camp, and my hunter and I would fly camp with a small Baker Tent. I would travel light and with few horses' ease up close to the Rams and stay well hid in the upper end of the valleys. Every hunter that I guided at Gary's, got their Ram and Goat, if they had tags for other animals, they came next. First we filled the important tags.

I had very few hunters with grizzly tags, and quite frankly saw little sign up in sheep country. When we dropped down into the timber, we would see tracks, but not many.

 *Stone Sheep near Blue Lake*

Some fine Stone Rams in the top two Photos and Getting horns ready to ship in the bottom

My First Stone Ram   *Mickey Simpson & I*

58 Inch Moose taken on Samuel's Mountain

One year a hunter by the name of Mel asked me if I had seen seen many bear? He mentioned that once we got passed the Ram and Goat, that he would sure like to try for a grizzly if we had time. I indicated that I had seen nothing all year. Once we connected with the Ram and goat, we did have time and went up to the Plateau overlooking Blue Lake and the Muskwa.

I set up a small camp with only four horses in a meadow of the side of the plateau. We took a wrangler to take care of the horses, the view was unbelievable, and would turn out to be my favourite camp through the years. Its amazing how animals can make a liar out of you, because that trip, this hunter had shots at five different Grizzlies before connecting on the sixth.

The first Grizzly was right in camp, one early morning, I opened the tent flap, and there he was standing on his hind leg twenty yards in front of the tent. I tapped the hunter still in bed, and he rolled over to see a large Silvertip staring at us. He fired right from his bedroll, and missed. The bear dropped on all fours, and was drifting down the hillside in leaps and bounds.

The hunter was so excited, that he started to jump out of his bedroll, almost took the tent and tent pegs, and gave chase. Finally he fell flat on his butt in a pile of willows. I hollered ¨´Whoa there pard´´, the bear was already half a mile away and heading out faster than my hunter could run, even in his long johns he would not be able to keep up.

He was so disappointed that he had missed, and even more so that day, because he missed another that evening. There were four more Grizzlies before he finally settled down. I will pass on to the number six Grizzly that he finally connected with.

Pete, Mel, Myself, and Connie Powell.

This is Grizzly number six

There was a young wrangler by the name of Pete that had joined us; the three of us had ridden over to a draw, just of the Plateau. We had the horses tied up to some willows and were glassing the ridge in front of us. I remember Pete asking for a chew of tobacco while we were glassing the country and had turned green in the process of chewing the stuff, it was a matter of time and he was pretty sick.

I noticed some movement a half a mile away with the binoculars; here was Grizzly number six coming up the pass from Blue Lake to the Muskwa. We got on our horses and rode over to the trail he was on and head him of. I asked Pete if he would take the horses, and wait down in the trees about five hundred yards bellow us and wait for the shooting before he came up.

Of he went, and my hunter and I waited on the trail for the bear to get a little closer to us. We did not have to wait long about twenty minuets, and here he came. He was digging roots along the trail and was all by

113

himself. That was good, and my hunter put the crosshairs on him, but I asked him not to shoot until I told him so.

He acknowledged he heard me and waited for my signal, I made sure that this time he did not mess up, as we were running out of bears and time.

The bear stopped right in front of us and began eating a root he was only about 75 yards from us, and down hill. I made this hunter watch him for a good ten minuets before asking him to put the cross hairs once again on his shoulder. He knew what he had to do, and finally quite shaking. I could tell from his rifle barrel that maybe he was ok now.

Then the big guy turned broadside and I told the hunter to take the shot if he felt good about it.

I told him to hit him right in the shoulder and break him down. The shot was made, and the bear dropped without any movement, he did not even twitch. We waited a few minutes, and went on down. The hunter had shot him dead in his tracks, the bullet was not in his shoulder, but behind his ear, no wonder he dropped.

Finally he connected with Bear No six

Caribou that we had not noticed coming in behind us, and they went running down the side hill right into Pete who was holding our horses. He was scared it was the Grizzly coming through the bush; we heard a blood-curdling scream and saw horses going everywhere. The hunter was happy, after some fifteen bear hunts, he finally landed one. He was a nice Boar about 600 lbs and a very pretty brown colour with blue guard hairs. I skinned him out, and proceeded to camp with a very happy hunter and sick wrangler.

This hunter had the gods in his favour, as he later also got a very nice Six Point Elk and 57 inch Bull Moose. It was quite common to get five species of animals, but not that easy to get five very good trophy heads on one hunt. He was a very lucky hunter.

I always liked this camp and over the years took several fine Billy's Moose and Caribou. I never did see any more Grizzlies that year.

Myself with Mel and his ram. On the far right is Doug Wiebe with his hunter Blue Lake 1972

Carl Vig &myself

Some fine Stone Rams, Moose and elk

Garry Powell had the finest Stone Sheep hunting in the Province.
He limited his Rams to just over twenty per year. That always
allowed for the harvesting of some fine Rams.

Top: Dr Harry 'Pusso' Morris with his fine Ram from Samuel's Mountain

Bottom: A young hunter packing out his Goat

Having the time of my life with this Sicilian Hunter whom had just moved to the USA. I knew he was definitely a Mafia Boss from the way he talked about everything and life in general.

He indicated to me that he had six shells and five tags, and that last shell was for me if I did not fill the tags. I did not really know if he was kidding around or serious. Whatever, he was a good shot and only used five shots on five animals.

I remember when he shot his Ram; we had spotted it right from the trail that we were riding our horses on. He shot the ram from beside his horse; it fell down the hill to within twenty yards of the trail. When I shook his hand to congratulate him, he said "Listen to me, I do not like all this walking, so get the next one a little closer ok".

I knew then he was fooling around. I would like to think that anyway.

Main Valley near the Forks. This is probably the largest Caribou that I have taken in the North.

Three nice full curls at the Gathto

The Hunting season for the year was about over. It was time to roll up my bedroll, and head South. I said all my goodbyes and jumped in the Cessna 180 and headed for Ft St John. Gary dropped me of and caught a Greyhound Bus down to Clinton. I did not drive back then, everywhere I went was with a Greyhound bus.

From there, I headed down to Pendleton to see all the friends I had made earlier. It always was a pleasure telling my friends all the thrills and adventures of that hunting season. Over the years the town of Pendleton became my second home. I loved the country and the people. One particular man by the name of Orval McCormmach who I consider to be one of my closest friends and who I was in Chile with when I decided to write this book, approached me at the saddle shop, It was full of Rodeo cowboys from all over the States and Canada.

He shouted out so everyone could hear " Hey there big game guide, all you talk about is skinning this or that, why don't you skin this and show us how its done." Orval had brought up to the saddle shop a Coyote that he had shot that morning. He had just declined an offer of seventy –five dollars for its pelt. He was really proud of this coyote that he felt was worth much more than the price offered. He kept running of at the mouth and so I took it down stairs to the Hide Room, that is where all the saddle trees are made. I cut this coyote into five quarters without skinning it. In less than one minute, I returned to the saddle shop with all the quarters in a box. Orval replied, "Boy that was fast, I guess you know what you are doing after all." Then I took the head out and threw it on the floor, this was followed by a couple of hindquarters all had the hide on.

He was furious and shouted at me saying," What the hell have you done to my coyote, I just turned down seventy –five dollars for it". And went stomping for the front door mad as hell. I shouted to him "Orval, I am not sure if I have done this right, as I am more familiar with skinning bigger animals," as he walked away. I hollered, "Don't forget your coyote", He never turned around or even looked back. He was very rude. I just hate rude behaviour in a man.

It was just a few days after that when I made it all up to Orval.and he got his money back.

Orval had a nice Bay Stallion that he had purchased from the Four 6666"s Ranch in Texas. His name was "Georges Top" he was out of the last direct daughter of "Joe Reed" and had good Hancock breeding on the other side. This horse was one of the finest horses that I had ever seen. Orval, Loren Wood, Duff Severe and Ike Rude had flown down to look the studs over and finally agreed on "Georges Top"

One day he asked me to accompany him on up to his Ranch. Orval said that a man was arriving to look the young foals over and possibly buy one. The stud was pasture breeding about fifteen mares and was somewhere out in this large pasture.

The man represented Chuck Shepard who was quite a famous cowboy from the South. I believe it was his brother in law. They had heard about the stud and wanted to see what type of colts he threw.

Orval asked me to go one way to look for "George" while they went the other.

I walked about half a mile and spotted him with all his mares down in a draw. I walked up to the stud and took my belt of my jeans and put it around his neck and jumped up on his back. The mares and foals were soon in a fast gallop up the draw to the barn. When we arrived, the mares tried to make a break for it and get by me. George was like a cat and cut them of and came to a sliding stop in front of these men. He did it all with just my belt around his neck.

I found out later that the man was so impressed with the way "George" performed that day that he bought all 15 foals right there and then.

So everything that goes around comes back around. Orval lost out on a coyote deal but sold 15 quality foals a week later worth many thousands and I never got a penny. Guess that taught me a lesson

Orval was good friends with a man from Las Vagas by the name of Benny Binion.

Mr Binion had a Ranch in Montana and asked Orval if he would be interested in Taking his high powered "Cutter Bill" stud for a few years and he would take "Georges Top" to put some new blood in each others stock.

After the third year, Orval called Mr Binion and said that he would like to bring his "Cutter Bill" stud back and pick up "George". I guess Mr Binion said that he could bring his horse back, but he wanted to buy "Georges Top". He offered Orval a very large sum of money for "George." Orval said that he would have to discuss it with his three daughters Kelly, Connie and Terry who are all very fine Horse Women themselves. They did not want to sell "George". This message was relayed to Mr Binion the next day. Mr Binion came back and doubled his offer and said that was as high as he would go.

Orval replied, " Mr Binion, you just bought a horse".

She's downhill and in the shade

CHAPTER EIGHT

W.D. Dingler and R.G. Pierce

While I was In Pendleton, A man offered me a job working with Thoroughbred Colts in a town called Klamath Falls, Oregon.

His name was R.G. Pierce. I went down there with him, and saw his operation. The training facility and barn was right adjacent to the racetrack in Klamath Falls. He had some of the finest Thoroughbreds and bloodlines that I had seen. Thoroughbreds were all new to me. Working with them was little different than any other colt. They were all babies; these ones were just a little feistier and better bred.

I also met at the time another man called W.D. Dingler. Both these men put together some twenty head of young two year olds for me to work with. Come spring, I had most all of them going quite well.

I started them all in a stock saddle, and then went into a saddle to gallop them with at the track. I had gained a little weight then, and weighed in at about 150 lbs, this was a perfect weight for a Gallop Boy as I was later to find out.

I was asked to join them in Portland in the early spring for the Races. Of I went to Portland with a whole bunch of young race colts.

Most of them did not pan out, but there were a few that could run a hole in the wind and did well that year.

Both they men knew their stuff around the racetrack, and proved to be masters of the game.

R.G Pierce had some very nice older horses that I got to gallop. Several were good enough for the California tracks and he was very good with bad horse's legs, especially thrush, and several people sent their horses to R.G with major hoof problems, which he cured over the winter.

The guy that I admired and watched so close was W.D.Dingler; he was a short guy, always had a Roi Tan cigar in his mouth and constantly complained about high prices. I only saw him claim one horse while I was with him. It was a horse called Mustedie. He complained that he was paying too much for him; He stopped complaining after the horse won four races for him that year and several seconds.

This man spent very little on the purchase of a race horse, the barn was always full of bad legged horses, matter of fact his horses had every major problem known to man with their legs.

W.D, would take the fever out of their legs, and run them on the bottom, right down their throats. We had no problem with anyone wanting to claim them, when they looked at their legs they quickly backed of. Sometimes he would bandage the good leg, and leave the bad one exposed for anyone to see. He loved his horses.

In 1969, we were leading trainers. I like to say we, because I was doing most all the Galloping. Actually, I was his assistant. The horses that made him the leading trainer were several good old campaigners, such as Foam Rubber, Easter Sam, Morning Smog, Bruele, Highlighter, Red Tartan and Mustiede. These were the backbone to his stable, and made him a lot of money that spring. One morning while I was going to the cookhouse for breakfast, I saw the meat wagon loading a horse. I asked the trainer what horse he was and he said it was 'Chicks Count' I had remembered this horse beating us in a race and when he came from off the pace, he flew. I asked the trainer, his name was Ysedro Bicandi what he was getting for the horse at the meat plant and he said fifty dollars. I offered him fifty-five dollars to save his life. I gave him the cash, and he gave me the horse and his papers. We did not have room for him, as all our stalls were full of good old hard runners. I had to rope of the cement walls in the manure pile. My plans were to send him to Pendleton and give him to the kids of a friend. It would be a while before they could come and get him, so I cared for him in the manure pile

. Dingler and I sat down one day and looked him over. What the hell, he had a Suspensory, a Bow, and several chips out of one leg. He was no worse of than all the rest of the boys and girls in the shed row. We decided to run him.

I started to gallop Chicks Count in the early morning, when it was still dark. He was very hard to hold at first, and pulled like a freight train. I could hold him and after a few gallops, he forgot all that and acted like a good boy. We went two mile gallops very slowly, what we call a hobbyhorse and were trying to get some air in him. His legs were the worst I had seen on a horse, and Dingler being the expert he was, soon got the fever out and Chicks Count was now in training.

The first time Bicandi saw his name on the form, he was quite mad, but he sold the horse to me, and that was that. He would be even madder after he ran his first race.

Chicks Count was entered going a mile and an eighth he drew in with some very tough horses, matter of fact, the horse that held the track record going that distance was in the race also. There was no way Chicks Count could outrun this guy, never in a million years. The horses name was Don Bob John.

What happened was a bit of sheer luck, as it rained and rained day and night before the race. This mud is what Chicks Count needed for those legs of his along with a slow pace.

The two-mile gallops paid of, he broke dead last and at the eighth pole, he was so far behind, I thought he had broke down. Then he started to move up, and in a whirl of mud and horses, he was in the lead. Chicks Count won by six lengths. What a horse. .

He went to Pendleton, and was turned out on the Mountain belonging to my friend Orval McCormmach and never ran again. It was a happy ending for a fifty-five dollar investment. Oh yes, I bet on him at the windows, and he paid like a slot machine.

I was in big demand at Portland with the colts. Several people knew that I was riding Broncs and when there was a nasty colt, they would call me.

They were not all that bad really, they were only two-year-olds, but often people would try and hurry them into their training, and they would start throwing everyone off.

Never in Portland's Meadows history have they seen a horse started out of the gate with a bronc saddle.

This one filly was dumping everyone, and I was called in to work with her.

Every time she went to the gate, she loved to buck and when she came out of the gate, she flew to bucking.

I rode her over to the gate in my Turtle Bronc saddle and bronc chaps, I had a snaffle bit in her mouth and just took it easy with her. I entered the starting gate and the starter by the name of Red asked me what was I going to do.

I told him to open the gate and I would trot her out. She blew up and I whacked her bum. Back in she went and the same happened. This went on until she finally quite all this nonsense. Then we tried the bell; she did not like that either, but got used to it. I only had to do this a couple of times, and we had her in a flat saddle working like a trooper. Her name was Beta Cola and won her first race by five lengths. The people that owned her were the Davis Family and they were thrilled at their baby.

Beta Cola winning the first time starter. She went on to be a very nice racehorse

The only two class horses that I got to gallop were called "Biscet" and "Spanculis"; Biscet was a great mare, and one of the few mares to win the Portland Meadows Mile.

Every winter for the next three years, I was down there starting all that years' crop. When I was through with Guiding Hunters, I would head down to Pendleton, and on to Klamath Falls.

It was that year that W.D won five races with five starters in one night. Everything we led over there won by six lengths. A couple of trainers jokingly asked what we were giving them to make them run so well. W.D replied, it is all in the feed, all in the feed.

The horses were all tucked away for the night and W.D said that he would treat the jockey and myself to a steak dinner, so out on the town we went. After we ate a great meal, W.D said he was not feeling good, and went out and sat in his pickup. He was feeling ok; he just didn't want to pay for the bill. He would do this to us all the time. W.D owned half the countryside around Klamath Falls, and was so tight with his money, he squeaked.

Highlighter Winning at Portland Meadows myself on the left.

W.D. Dingler holding the horse

One other occasion, we had two winners in a night, once again; he was going to treat us. This time he wanted to buy a jacket for the evening.

Where did we shop? The Salvation Army. We went in, and he found a jacket, there was some loose change in the lining. He bought the jacket for 25 cents, went outside, took his pocket knife and cut the lining, took out forty cents from the jacket and returned the jacket a few minuets later saying it was too tight. They gave him a refund.

This was my boss, and I loved to watch him do these crazy things.

One thing for sure, W.D. Dingler knew how to get the run out of those bad-legged horses.

She's downhill and in the shade

CHAPTER NINE

Vold Rodeo and Jay Sissler

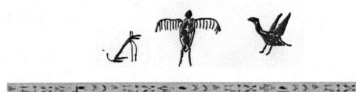

Things went on as usual, I went to all the Rodeos that Vold and Kessler put on that summer. They were the two top Stock Contractors in Alberta. This season was a little different though, as Glen Randall was not up in Canada. I was offered a job working with Jay Sissler.

Jay was the greatest dog trainer I have ever seen. He had a dog act that brought the house down at the rodeos. I helped him in the act, while I rode Saddle Broncs at the rodeos.

He had three dogs and a greyhound that were the act. There was Doc, Silver, Sparky and one other. They had a very comical act, full of laughs that the crowd loved. I toured all that summer with Jay and it was a very memorable one. I would receive a letter and a card from him every year. He got married and lived in Emmett Idaho. One year, I did not receive anything, and later, I heard from his wife, that he had passed away. Travelling with Jay and his dogs was truly an experience that I will never forget. Many people that saw his dog act consider it to be the best ever performed.

Jay with Silver and Doc

She's downhill and in the shade

Sarcee Sorrel's Debut

The horses bucked as good as the year before if not better. Between Rodeos, I went to help Wayne Vold with some bucking horses in DeWinton. This was a small town outside of Calgary. He had told Jerry Poncelet and myself to go down to the Sarcee Indian Reservation, as someone down there had run four young horses into a corral, right of the open range. Wayne wanted to try them out. We took Wayne's younger brother Doug down with us; he was only about 12 or 13 years old. When we were figuring out a plan on how we were going to load two of them in a two-horse trailer at the corral, Doug opened the trailer door, grabbed a stock whip, and chased the colts down the alley into the trailer and closed the door.

He said, "No problem boys, they are loaded let's go home. These two young colts had never seen a corral before let alone a horse trailer. They jumped in there like they had been hauled a million miles. What a kid he was. He later went on to be a fine bronc rider and for many years had the highest marked Bronc Ride in Canada. I do not know if that record stands today.

Doug "Scrufty" Vold with Pendleton Rodeo Queen Julie Rugg. Scrufty won the Saddle Bronc Riding at Pendleton in 1976 and a fully hand carved bronc saddle made by Severe Bros.

Wayne gave the horse a name, it was Sarcee Sorrel and his debut was at the Kids High School Rodeo in the next town by DeWinton. I believe it was called Okatoks. When the gate opened and Sarcee Sorrel came out of the cute, not only did he throw the High school kid of that day, he bucked as hard as the Canadian Champion Bucking mare Necklace. I have not seem a horse buck so hard as Sarcee Sorrel the first time he came out of the chute gate. Wayne was screaming at the top of his voice at the pickup men to get the flank off. Finally Sarcee Sorrel let them come close enough to trip the flank. Everyone knew he was an outstanding bronc.

His career as a bucking horse was a long one, and there were thousands of dollars won on him. There were very few qualified rides on him.

I got on some great bucking horses that year, and made many good friends. Denton Moffat from Hussar, Alberta invited me to his fathers ranch between rodeos. Denton had a bucking horse that he practised on. He was an amazing good old horse, because he would just stand there in the chute while Denton did everything on his back. He would flank him, push the gate open and then, when he wanted to stop bucking he would say "Whoa" and trip the flank. The horse would stop, and he would get of and lead him back.

He took me into his workshop, and I saw he was building his own saddle; He was a very talented man, and a very tough bronc rider to beat. I helped Denton work a few colts while I was there and showed him some of the things that I would do when starting young horses. Things that I had learned from Loren Wood and Duff Severe. Denton went on to become a tough competitor in The Cutting Horse scene. He then went on to study and become one of the top Horse Vets in British Colombia. It was a good year, and I really did enjoy Alberta.

She's downhill and in the shade

CHAPTER TEN

Back to Garry Powell's

That fall took me back up to Gary Powell's Outfitting for another successful year. The game was plentiful, and I had noticed that the Elk were spreading out further and further than Gathto Creek. We were starting to see them in areas that they had never been seen before. Every place I went in the fall, I was hearing Elk Bugle. All the years that I worked there, it was rare to see a five point elk come in to camp. Every hunter would get a six pointer. We would take some thirty to forty six pointers a year out. Almost all my sheep hunters would shoot an elk. Normally they were not that interested, but when you see a large six pointer in front of you, it's a little hard to resist. The rams were plentiful, and I got all my hunters some very respectable heads. I saw a very large ram that year up in Powell Creek. He was the largest ram I had seen there in all the years of guiding there. He was also the smartest, and did not take any chances. He had his eyes open and constantly looking for anything suspicious. The storms were coming in from the north and must have moved him out. I spent several days spotting and searching all the areas that I would normally pick him up. He must have been passing through the country.

A Hunter, Mickey Simpson and I at base Camp on the Gathto River

A fine batch of Stone Sheep Horns

Bottom picture is one of the largest six pointers that I have ever got

Some fine Rams and a large Moose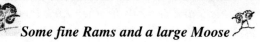

Nice Six Point elk taken on the Muskwa

Top left: Our young wrangler, who later in life lost his life in a plane wreck. Two hunters and Garry's brother Jack Powell on the right
Bottom left: Caribou on Samuel's Mountain

It was that year that I met at base camp the Wrangler who was on the Hunt when the Chadwick Ram was taken some fifty years ago. This stone ram is considered to be the finest stone sheep head of all.

This man was quite elderly and had flown in with Gary to spend a few days at the lodge. I always enjoy talking with these guys; they are so interesting and have sure paid their dues in the mountains.

Gary once told me that he used to pick up a prospector in the late fall after a whole summer of wondering through the mountains. This guy had two large Husky dogs that he packed. This one fall he was there at the designated spot, they loaded the dogs and the prospector and proceeded down the runway on a dirt strip. As they were about to get airborne, the two huge huskies decided to get into a scrap in the plane. The fight was on. Garry had to quickly turn the aircraft around and land again before they damaged the whole interior. I guess they wrapped their muzzles the next time, and the prospector sat on the instigator. From then on everything went well. I don't recall him ever saying he took him out again.

The Elk horns in the shed at the Gathto

One of my favourite rams, taken in Powell Creek

Acquiring this ram was one of the scariest moments of my life. As we were crawling along a ledge, the hunter jabbed me in the butt with a rifle barrel. I asked him politely if that rifle had the safety off and a shell in the chamber. He replied it did. I read him the riot act and the stalk ceased.

140

Prime Sheep Country near the Forks

I was in the mountains with a hunter that I had been with the year before. He was a doctor from Missouri and a great guy; I remember he was a heart specialist, because he always examined the hearts of all the animals we took.

Anyway, we had filled our tags right up; he got a beautiful ram and goat along with a very large moose and elk. All there was to do was to wait and glass this mountain for a grizzly. We had a lot of time on our hands.

Gary had mentioned earlier if I might be able to get him a Bighorn from my hometown area down south. The season was very short down there, and soon it would be over. Now was the time to ask my doctor, if he would be so kind as to give me a few days of from his hunt to take the boss down for a Bighorn. It takes a lot of gall to ask the hunter of this, especially when he has paid thousands of dollars for this hunt, and now I am off with somebody else.

I told the doc, that I would need three days to do it. That included the flights down and back. His answer was ¨´ If you think you can leave here, ride 10 miles on a horse, jump in a Super cub, then in a 180 Cessna and fly to Clinton some five hundred miles away Shoot a California Bighorn Ram and return in three days, you got it.

That's exactly what we did and in three days, we buzzed Docs camp tilted our wings, dropped a message saying ´´we did it the evening of the third day, I was back with Doc on the mountain and my boss had a nice Bighorn.

Fall Hunting was coming to an end; I finished up with my last hunter, and pulled the saddle of Roger and turned him out for the winter. It was time to head on down to Clinton, spend some time with all my friends, and head on down to Pendleton to see my old pards. 🖐

 Garry Powell's ram in the Limestone's out of Clinton

She's downhill and in the shade

CHAPTER ELEVEN
The OK Ranch

There was a fresh batch of colts waiting for me in Klamath Falls. I knew sooner than later, I would be there for the winter. Then on to Portland Meadows for another season of Racing With W.D.Dingler and R.G.Pierce.

Before I left for the south, I went out to help Jean Park who was now the owner of the OK Ranch on the banks of the Fraser River. Jean was one of the first guys that I met when I arrived in Clinton Years ago. Floyd Grinder, his brothers Ralf and Roy were there also. I helped round up all the cows in the late fall. I enjoyed helping Jean whenever I could, and the ranch was a magnificent piece of real estate over looking the Fraser River and Big Bar Mountain.

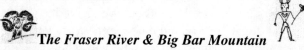

The Fraser River & Big Bar Mountain

That fall, when I was looking in one of the older buildings at the ranch, my foot went through a floorboard, it was half-rotten. When I went to pull it out, the board lifted, and I saw a stack of old letters.

It was impossible to read the top and bottom ones, because they had deteriorated very badly. The centre one was in excellent condition, and was dated in the 1930˜'s they were all a stack of love letters from a guy by the name of Herb Metier to a lady who's last name was Dougherty. This particular letter was from her and she was giving him the brush-off saying that he did not mean this and that, and that she never wanted to see him again. For some reason, I never destroyed them; I just put them back under the floorboards.

The next year, I dug them out again, because this Herb Metier was a legend in his time, was in his 90˜'s and was going to officially open the Williams Lake Rodeo. It was priceless as we arrived at the Rodeo to compete; we had this letter in hand dated some forty years earlier, had given it to the announcer Bud Stewart who was a good friend and he chuckled after reading it. After Herb officially opened the rodeo with his huge ten-gallon hat, Bud called Herb and said that a letter had arrived for him, and proceeded to lower it tied to the microphone.

We were all watching from the bucking chutes, as he took out his spectacles and began to read. He jumped back, regrouped, and continued to read. When it was all over, he folded his spectacles, folded the letter put them in a pocket chuckled and then walked away. He didn't even look up or around, just chuckled and walked away bet he never thought that letter would ever surface or where it even came from.

While we were at the OK, a man by the name of Joe Kelsey arrived.

He was a Stock Contractor from Washington and was snooping around BC looking for bucking horses.

Floyd and Jean told him there were several out at Big Bar and would not take them long to bring in for him to see.

There were several bronc riders around, Roy and I were eager to get on a few and so we did just that.

There were about four in all that we bucked and the best one to buck was a berry pickin mare that belonged to Bert Grinder. She was a grey mare and could flat ass buck. I told Bert one could loose all your berries if she decided to have a bad day. Joe brought out the whiskey and before the afternoon had passed, he had a couple of the horses loaded. One was the grey mare that everyone used to pick berries on.

The next time I saw her was at Calgary for the stampede.

A cowboy from the states drew her and I told him what she had done when I rode her. He was all ready and had his saddle on her and when the chute gate opened, she did exactly what I said she would do.

He picked himself out of the ground and she claimed another victim.

I drew a great saddle bronc that year at Williams Lake and when he came out of the cute, de drifted over to the fence and was making his mind up about whether to go to the left or right. It was about then, that I heard this tremendous roar, somebody said near the fence" turn your toes out" It was a voice I had heard so many times before, and startled me. It was Wayne Robinson. I rode the horse and split a second on him. Soon as I got of the horse I went and sat with him and his wife. He was thrilled that I had got them for a second, but said if I would have turned my toes out better, I could have won First.

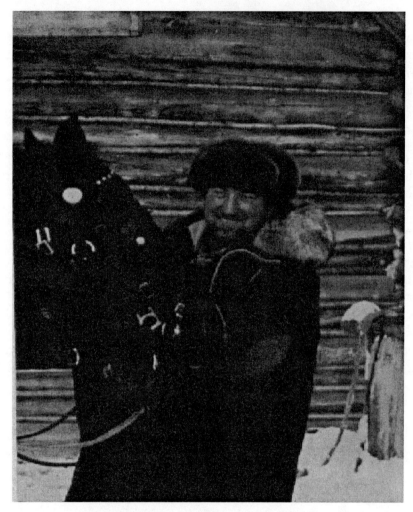

Myself at the Ok Ranch in -20 bellow

Anyway now that I told that story. All the Cattle were rounded up, and the buyers were there at the OK Corrals. They liked Jeans calves, because they were so even and hard. The Fraser and Big bar mountain was sure the place to run cows. It was the next year that I would be back up at Jeans for the branding on Big bar Mountain in mid summer.

Fraser River near the OK Ranch

Roy Grinder shoeing a horse at the Ok Ranch

Jean, Floyd and myself were returning from branding and we were riding back to the ranch buildings. Jean and myself were riding two colts, they were full brother and sister, one was called big bar, the other slips my mind, and Floyd was riding a big Buckskin Gelding that was very well broke.

We rounded the mountain by Stinkin Lake, and there right in front of us was this very large brown bear. It was the bear that had killed a calf a week earlier. That time we had no rifle with us, and had watched him chase a young calf. Later that night he caught one. There was nothing left of the calf come morning.

Anyway, here we had him right in front of us with at least five hundred yards of open flat on each side of the valley. Once again, we did not have a rifle

We got of our horses and re-set our saddles with a tight cinch. I went to the right side of the bear in case he decided to go downhill and to the right, Jean went in the middle, and Floyd took the left side, we had our ropes down and off we went.

The bear did not know anything until we were about 100 yards from him, he must have heard the noise of three large horses thundering down on him. He stood up on his hind legs briefly, then dropped and started to run up the hill. Floyd was the first one on him, and before the buckskin gelding knew what he had done, Floyd roped him deep around his chest. You should have heard this bear roar as the rope tightened up. Neither Jean nor I could get our young colts close enough to catch a hind leg with this bear roaring and on the fight. Here Floyd was with a large bear, and his horse did not like it one bit. Matter of fact, he started to buck, and Floyd had to turn him loose.

We chased him up the ridge and he climbed a large fir tree. Now we all sat on our horses watching the bear sit on a large limb chewing Floyd's good rope that was around his chest and shoulder. He had about two strands chewed in half when Floyd could not stand it any longer. He got of his horse went under the tree and tugged on the lariat that was hanging down. Soon as he tugged, the bear crapped all over him. That did it with Floyd, first the Bear eats a Calf, and then eats his rope, and now craps all over him.

This bear was not getting away, as we all drew straws to see who was going to ride back and get a rifle, and who was going to stay and keep him up the tree.

I stayed and kept him in the tree. The bear never killed a calf again, and we never had any more calves disappear. Floyd had to get in the bath tub, then get a new lariat, and life continued on Big bar Mountain.

I was considering getting into judging the Rodeos, as there was one on every weekend throughout the summer. Floyd and Jean Park were going to every one so I went to the association and applied for the job. They put me through a judging class. I passed and here I was judging my first rodeo. I had watched very closely what the Judges needed to see for the high scores. I had been around enough good stock to know what to look for in a Bucking Horse and Bull

 As it would turn out, there were about twelve rodeos a year that I would do. And was even elected to judge the finals In Williams Lake one year. I remember having to flag out my good friend Floyd Grinder on a steer one day. The rules called for the contestant to throw the steer. Well the steer actually tripped and fell. I rode up and told Floyd to let him up and throw him correctly. Floyd asked for a flag, and I gave him one, I flagged him out.

He turned to me, and said are you forgetting whom you are travelling with.

When the cowboys saw this, they saw that I was pretty darn honest and would not favour any of my mates. Even the ones I was travelling with. There is one thing for sure about judging a rodeo; you have few friends when you go, and fewer when you leave.

Big Bar Mountain in the dead of winter

The Ok Ranch is one of the finest ranches in BC. It runs along the Fraser River, and has excellent spring and fall range

She's downhill and in the shade

CHAPTER TWELVE

THE DOUGLAS LAKE CATTLE COMPANY

While I was at The Williams Lake Rodeo, there was some major Cutting going on with the all the top Cutting Horses in the country. I was approached by a man called Mr C.N Woodward and was offered a job working some young colts at his Ranch. I had seen him and his horses at all the major cuttings. I always admired the quality of horse he rode, two of them were World Champion Cutting Horse's one by the name of ´Peppy San´, and the other was Stardust Desire. He said he was from The Douglas Lake Ranch, which I already knew.

I had to politely decline his offer, I told Mr Woodward that I was about to spend the summer riding bucking horses and could not do it at the moment. I was also a little upset that 10 years earlier the Douglas Lake Ranch did not answer my letter when I really wanted to work on a Ranch after I got out of school. Now here we are a few years later and the ranch is asking me if I wanted a job.

In the spring of 1972 while I was at the Kamloops Rodeo, Mr Woodward approached me again, this time I accepted.

I wrapped up a lot of odds and ends that I had to do in Clinton, and told W.D. Dingler that I would not be down this spring to Gallop at Portland meadows for him.

Driving through to Merritt B.C was very similar to the Gang Ranch and Empire Valley, the rolling bunchgrass was everywhere.

I arrived at the ranch and was met by Dave Bade who was the Cutting Horse trainer there. He showed me to a nice trailer that was to be home.

The facility was very impressive with large corrals and a huge indoor arena. I was introduced to the Colts and there were seven, all of them were geldings and all were two year olds.

The next day, I ran them all into the round pen together, and watched their reaction with me in the pen with them. These colts were not pampered along as yearlings, hand fed and spoilt. They all turned away from me and kept their distance.

Then, I separated the colts one at a time, and watched their reaction with them one on one in the round pen. They had a halter on them when they were yearlings, and had not been touched since. It does not take me very long to figure out all the little signals they send you to saying‘‘ hey pard, I'm ready to co-operate’’ and the ones that say ‘‘come near me and Ill plant your butt’’ they were all pretty good and I new I was going to have fun with these guys. A man who had started Peppy San colts had told me earlier, that they were all quite broncy.

From what I was looking at, did not hold water. What I did see, was the best-bred and best-looking batch of colts I ever had the privilege of starting. I could not wait to begin.

As in every batch of colts one works with, there are the smart ones, and the real smart ones. Everything you do with a colt, you have to appeal to his memory and it does not take a person long to see which colts are faster learning than others are. If the Preperation is done correctly, the exercise comes much easier. I like to spend a lot of time doing my groundwork and flat work in a riding arena.

I have always incorporated a Lariet with my round pen work, thanks to Duff Severe and Loren Wood teaching me. If a person can handle a rope and does not miss, you can teach a horse a lot of manners. I hate a horse that turns his butt to you. He must learn right a way to face me and walk up to me without any fear of the rope, or me. The round pen and riding arena is the school and that is where the discipline comes into play with the schooling of a young colt.

These Peppy San colts were great to work with, there was not one colt that even offered to buck and the schooling progressed rapidly. They were and are to this day, the smartest colts I have ever started. I have started some well-bred colts over the years, but to date, these top the charts.

Now, let me tell you about two of them. One of the Colts was called ¨´Royal Santana¨´, and the other was called ¨¨Booger San¨. These colts were only two years old and had a mind like no other colts.

They were very quick to learn and very eager to please. It seemed they wanted to do nothing wrong. The three things that are needed with a young horse is a horse that is obedient, supple and quite. From there you build and made a good horse. Without one of those three things, it is impossible to finish a horse or move on to any sort of high school Riding.

These colts learned the discipline fast and were very obedient and above all, they were quite. That no doubt came from the good breeding of Peppy San. And his quality mares.

One fine day after 60 days of schooling, Mr Woodward with the Minister of Finance for the Province a Mr Stupich along with The General Ranch Manager Mr Mike Ferguson walked down to see how I was doing at the Cutting Horse barn. I asked them to follow me to the huge indoor arena, and to be as quite as possible.

At the far end was a colt saddled up with a very light hackamore on, it was Royal Santana. I walked into the arena, and called him and said ¨´come here. This colt came at a gallop down to me from the other end and stopped right beside me. I did not have to move one step, and I put a foot in the stirrup and got on. I warmed him up and did some nice flat work and lead changes, stops and a very nice back up.

Then as a last exercise, I brought him down the centre and asked for a nice stop. He planted his but in the ground. He was so light in the hackamore and did it perfectly. I told Mr Woodward, that this was the finest colt I had ever ridden. I got of and loosened his cinch. In fact, he had his half brother Booger San that was equally as smart watching the whole show. The only difference between them both was their colour.

I had more and more fun working with these seven colts, but most of all, it was these two. I have yet today to start two smarter colts. It was several years later that I was told of their achievements. Dave Badey approached me, and asked if I knew what had happened to these two young colts that I was so high on many years ago at the Douglas lake ranch. I replied that I had not. He then proceeded to inform me of the records they had both set, with Royal Santana winning the World Championship and now being inaugurated to the Hall of Fame, a place with the greatest Cutting Horses of all time in the United States. The Bay colt Booger San was the second highest money earner of all the colts Peppy San had sired. Booger san was my favourite out of the two. I had wished they had kept them studs. They were stud material.

I knew in my heart the first day I ran them both in the corral, these two were destined to be champions, if they could go on to the right hands, without injury. They apparently did. It was a pleasure to start them.

Picture of Royal Santana at a Cutting Event with a professional trainer. This horse along with Booger San, are the two smartest Colts that I have ever had the opportunity of starting in my life.

Foaled in 1971, sired by Peppy San
Bred by Douglas Lake Cattle Co. Ltd. of British Columbia
Trained by Matlock Rose, Sonny Rice and Dave McGregor
Purchased by Frank Merrill of Purcell, Oklahoma, in 1985
AQHA youth high-point cutting horse, 1990
AQHYA world champion cutting horse, 1990
AQHA world champion amateur cutting horse, 1991
Died in 1995
Inaugurated to AQHA Hall of Fame

She's downhill and in the shade

CHAPTER TWELVE

COLD FISH LAKE/HYLAND POST

I had heard that there was a job opening in the North, and that the Spatzizi Hunting operation out of Smithers was looking for a manager.

I decided to see what this was all about, and before I knew it, I was headed for the Spatzizi.

The Owner was a man by the name of Howard Paish. Howard had an Environmental Consulting Company, and operated out of the lower mainland. He was a very intelligent man and had a very professional team working with him.

I sized the operation over, and there was no doubt about the Spatzizi, it was a large piece of Northern Real estate that was virtually untouched.

The area was remote, and one had to fly some 200 air miles to Cold Fish Lake from the town of Smithers. There was little or nothing as far as people between both places.

I liked the operation and its base camp at Coldfish. It was situated at the Northern end of the Lake and the lake was some 8 miles in length and very deep. The mountains surrounding Coldfish Lake were stupendous, with high alpine surrounding the entire area. It was a pretty sight to fly into.

A nice Bull Caribou

Down the Spatzizi some twenty miles was Hyland Post. It was the area and camp that was a lot lower in elevation and where all the horses wintered. A fine network of log cabins, and a large airstrip that was in good shape.

The horse herd consisted of about two hundred horses, of which many were not able to corral and thus little use to the operation. There were a couple of River Boats that were used for freighting on the Stikinne and Spatzizi rivers. All in all, it seemed like typical northern Operation that had Great fishing and excellent hunting.

As it turned out, the caribou hunting was undoubtedly the best that I had ever seen. There were vast herds of caribou and goats numbering upwards of a hundred or more on the high plateaus several, with very respectable horns. There was better than average moose with many in the high fifties.

My question is always, what have we got for rams? As it turned out, there were several very nice rams that were taken, they were spread out a lot, with stone sheep scattered over the entire area.

The largest Rams that I saw were overlooking the Stikinne and Spatzizi rivers.

I arrived at the operation several months before the actual fall hunting began. A lot of the horse herd had not seen a corral for several years, it also turned out that an outfitter who had the adjacent operation had used several horses.

I came back to Clinton and proceeded to buy some twenty-two good saddles and pack horses. I needed one full truckload. This was not hard to do, the country was full of good horses and I had my selection out of several hundred. Once the word got out, that I was buying horses, it did not take me long to put the herd together.

We needed a good Percheron stud, and were keeping my eyes open for one. The local R.C.M.P.Police had somebody in jail, I guess some hippy had taken up residence down along the Fraser River in no mans land, and had shot a couple of Bighorn Sheep to feed his family. He was going to do time, and be deported. Anyway, he had four horses, the police asked me if I could round his horses up. Low and behold, there was a two-year-old Percheron stud running with the others. I contacted the guy in jail, and he was a registered Percheron, and for sale.

I offered him 125 dollars, he took it and I paid his wife. Now we had a load of good solid horses, and a stud to start raising our string for the mountains. We loaded the herd into the commercial stock truck and trailer and headed up to Iskut on the Stewart Cassiar Highway. My price for the horses delivered to Iskut was 225dollars per horse. I thought I had done pretty well.

Once we unloaded them at Iskut, we still had a long way to go. We figured about five to six days of travelling to get them to Hyland Post. This was all in country that I had never been through. I had picked up a couple of young local boys from Iskut. They were going to give me a hand all the way to Hyland post. I also had a young lad from Ash croft and who turned out to be a great help on the whole trip, his name was Mike Nielsen. The horses were fantastic and performed like troopers they were quite and every one carried a small pack. When we reached the river one day out, the two local lads refused to cross the river. I said that we would wait until early morning, and head across when the river was low. I crossed the river twice to show them that it was not bad, they still refused saying it was to high. What could I do, as I was in a situation were I could not go ahead with just one young lad, and we could not go back.

I saddled the worst horse of the twenty-two, which was a roan mare, and headed back were I had come from. I then gave the horse to a guy that owned a store there, and hitchhiked up the highway to a place called Dease Lake. That's where the closest Jet Ranger Helicopter sat. We then went back, picked up the two who refused to cross the river, and ferried them across in a chopper.

Large Moose on The Spatzizi Plateau

Mike and I crossed the river while the pilot helped drive them in. We made it without any problems from there on in. This cost me a lot of extra time and money. It gave me an opportunity to see what kind of guides I was going to be working with, and I guarantee you, they would never work out in my camp. I followed the map and figured out the different mountain ranges as we moved ahead. The North is pretty simple to figure out, as it takes sometimes one whole day to ride up a valley. It is just a question of deciding which side of the valley has the best and most used caribou trail. We made it into Cold Fish Lake all the horse performed well. None of them even had a saddle sore, which made me feel even better. We spent the night there, and headed on down to Hyland Post the next day. We passed Scotty's Meadow and straight down the Spatzizi River to camp. I had noticed an Indian message tree along the route. I guess back in the old days, people from different areas, would carve a message in this huge tree and news got passed on that way. There was an older Indian village called Caribou Hide that had long been deserted, maybe this was the mail route through the mountains. Several of the old timers that worked at Cold Fish Lake had family that were raised in Caribou Hide. They told me that they used to pack the dogs in the summer, and sled them in the winter to get supplies to Caribou hide. It was good Grizzly country and several large bears were spotted in the area.

Large grizzly on the Plateau

She's downhill and in the shade

CHAPTER THIRTEEN

CREATING THE SPATZIZI PARK

I was informed by Howard Paish that a team of Government and Provincial Park Officials would be arriving at Cold Fish Lake along with them was the National Film Board crew who was going to film parts of the area and this event, There were experts here and experts there from botanists to geologists. My job was to take them around the mountains on horse back while the film board took the footage. There was a Jet Ranger Helicopter that was also used to carry equipment and the experts.

 I don't think Howard Paish knew just what was going on in these government officials' heads. Here we were assisting them in creating the largest ecological reserve and one of the largest Parks in the province. I remember standing just outside camera range and listening to the expert botanist explain (while he was being filmed) how rare certain plants were, and that he had never seen these plants growing anywhere in the north and for them to be on the Spatzizi Plateau was indeed very rare. This was getting too much for all of us to handle, and finally someone said, if you care to jump into the helicopter and fly to that huge plateau of to the north, you would see the same plants in abundance.

I heard more crap that day from people with degrees, who had never been to the north in their lives and here they are making decisions that would affect the entire area. As it was, the area was later made into the largest Ecological Reserve in Canada and the rest was of the area was tabled to be made into a very large Park.

I could see the handwriting was on the wall as far as any future hunting operation was concerned. It would all be coming to an end and the end was not that far away.

Things moved fast, and before we knew it fall was here and the hunters were arriving. Just 24 hours before the opening of the season, we incorporated a jet ranger helicopter to ferry all the various camps going out. All the tents and groceries went and the cook. We would then ride in with the hunters and wrangler the opening day. This freed up a lot of horses otherwise used as packhorses.

This one young gal from Vancouver was a cook on one of the camps being set up on the Spatzizi Plateau. It was her first time in the great outdoors, and was pretty green about all this, anyway, she was dropped off on the plateau, and we were all due to arrive the next day.

When we did arrive, it was in the afternoon, and we saw our tents had been put up and were all demolished, this gal, was up a tree and had been there for a long time.

She said that a grizzly had arrived in camp, and she climbed a tree and watched him destroy our camp.

She wanted to leave immediately, and asked for someone to escort her out. It took quite a bit of convincing, that this sort of thing never happens, and that it would never happen in a million years. Finally, she started to come around, and we had our cook back.

I sent a wrangler back to Cold Fish for a new set of tents, and we were back in business.

We connected on all the game we had tags for, and then something happened once again.

This time it was not a bear but a wolverine that came into her tent in the middle of the night. She slept in the 12x14 cook tent. It was about midnight that she came and crawled into the guide's tent, and asked to sleep with us. She had all her bedding and we asked what's the matter? She said there was something in her tent and she was not hanging around to see what it was. I got up and went to the cook tent. I thought it would be a Porcupine looking for salt. What was on the kitchen table was a large adult wolverine and he did not like anyone disturbing his meal.

I shot the wolverine, and quickly threw him into the bushes before the whole camp came to see what had happened.

I told the cook that it was a porcupine and that I had scared him away with a rifle shot. If she had seen the real culprit, she would have been packing her bags come morning, and been on the first horse heading south.

The next day, she said, " there was a strange odour in the cook tent" and she did not think porcupines had a foul urine smelling odour to them.

We quickly changed the subject and said something like we had to go hunting. One of the hunters went home with a nice wolverine hide.

 The Rams we got on that hunts were nice rams, they were not high scoring but any full curl ram is respectable, all the hunters were happy. I remember having my hunter out on a high rim overlooking some ledges. The rams were just below us and we were waiting patiently for them to start feeding out on a ledge, where we could get a decent shot.

While we were waiting, a nanny goat and this year's kid were grazing out on a ledge. They were occupying our time. Then, without any warning, there were four wolves on the same ledge as her. My hunter wanted a wolf in the worst way, but I told him that the ram was more important and not to shoot. I sure did not want to loose these rams over a wolf.

Anyway, we waited for Mother Nature to take its course and thought within seconds the wolves would have her strung out and make a meal of her and her kid. What happened next, was something I wish that I had on video. The wolves circled her and got her against a sheer wall, the young kid was under her belly and staying close to her, her hair on her back was straight up in the air and ready to do battle. The nanny had a set of eleven-inch horns and proved she knew how to defend herself.

The wolves worked her back and forth, and she held her ground not even moving an inch. One of the wolves made a pass at her, to try and grab the kid; she jumped ten feet sideways and buried her horns in his side. She immediately jumped back over her baby to protect it. Then what happened was even more bizarre, the injured wolf started to bite his own side and the other three wolves jumped on him and started a fight. It was as if they were going to scold him for messing up the kill.

While this commotion was going on, the nanny made a quick getaway with her kid, into some very rough and steep cliffs. I would never have believed something like this could have happened, unless you would see it with your own eyes. Half an hour later, we spotted the three wolves together, and the injured one trailing by a few hundred feet.

I would not have expected him to live, as there was blood, all over his side. That evening is when we connected on the ram.

That same hunter was very lucky with his moose and caribou. A few days later, we were on the Spatzizi Plateau, and I had spotted a very large moose, his rack was high fifty's. When we were making the stalk, we were just about in place, when we walked into a huge caribou that was laying down in a small draw. The hunter shot the very large bull caribou, and ran fifty yards up a small hill, and there was the fifty-nine in moose. He dropped the large moose with about twelve shots. This moose did not want to go down. I had two animals to cape and all the meat to pack in. The horses were about five hundred yards away and had all the quarters to pack in. This called for a busy day.

There were a lot of hunters booked that season, way more hunters than what we could handle. A lot of the horses had to be worked long hours, it was at this time, that some guide and wrangler were bringing pack horses up to Cold Fish Lake, when one of the horses went missing. He had a full load on, and had to be found. Normally when these sorts of things happen, every available person would be sent to the area to look for the horse. This did not happen; a brief search was made and dropped. This decision would all come back to haunt Howard in a court case a year or so later. Eventually the horse was found, it was a sorry sight to see, even though he had shed the pack, the saddle had turned, and the cinches had eaten into his back and withers and had swollen to a sight I will not forget.

I asked Bert Grinder to care for the horse, and he was now in good hands. Bert came up with me from Clinton, and was one of the best Indian cowboys in the area. He was getting on in years, but one could not find a better horseman. The horse had the rest he needed, and made a full recovery, and then was turned out.

I had several serious things happen that I did not approve of with the hired help; I wanted them on the next plane out of there. Howard said that he did not want to let them go, he was always giving me some cock and bull story about how we needed these guys and how their fathers had worked here before them. It was true, their fathers were the salt of the earth, and knew the Spatzizi inside and out. They were from a different school. I was batting my head against a brick wall, and knew I would not be in the Spatzizi as a foreman or assistant manager much longer.

One of the local guides from Iskut took a hunter into the Eagle Nest Range and set up camp. The hunter was a very professional sheep hunter that needed the Stone Ram to complete his grand slam.

The first day into camp, this guide goes out and shoots a young ram for camp meat. The hunter was furious, and complained that the larger rams had now left the area. The hunter said that he did not need camp meat, the rams that left the area.

I reported this incident to the boss, and I said that this guide has got to go right now, and that we cannot run a Hunting Operation with hired help like this. This guide was also one of the two that came in with me when I brought the 22 horses from Iskut. The guide stayed on.

Every time we turned around, we had people like this putting the operation in difficult situations. Ones that I personally was not accustomed to, and I could do nothing about.

More and more hunters were arriving at base camp. Even the Director of Fish and Game and The Director Of Ecological Reserves arrived for a hunt. They were packed up and into the mountains and left alone to fend for them selves. I remember Dr Hatter hunting with a bow and he was a very good shot. I cannot recall if either one had got anything, I don't think they did.

I knew that I would not be long with this operation, but did not expect a year later to be drug into a major court battle with Howard Paish and The Fish And Wildlife. It later turned out to be the largest investigation ever launched into an outfitter by the Game Department.

A few interesting events happened when I was up there. Apparently some guy had flown his plane across country heading for Smithers. He had bad weather, and crashed his plane on the top of a mountain. The pilot survived the crash; he then proceeded to work his way down the mountain to the Spatzizi River. He was pretty torn up, and had several injuries from the crash. He said he was following the river down, when he ran into a grizzly bear. The bear charged him and mauled him around, which led to even more injuries. The man jumped into the Spatzizi River and drifted down before coming out on the other side. This guy must have had nine lives, because the river is very cold, and one does not last very long in it.

Anyway, he made it to shore and walked down a trail. He said he saw a light. It was the cabin at Scotty's Meadow, there were two guys there rounding up horses. When this pilot banged on the door, he must have looked awful and was probably in shock. These two inside must have thought he was a mad man, and ran him off.

He drifted down the trail another 12 miles before coming to Hyland Post and safety. When he started to tell this story to us, he said that he was more scared of the guys at Scotty's Meadow than the Plane wreck, the bear or the river. We had him on a plane and out to hospital the next day.

It wasn't long after that when Ronnie Bruns Flew into Cold Fish Lake and hit a horse with his Cessna.185

The Wranglers job was to clear the runway every time a plane wanted to land. These two wranglers went out and one cleared the main strip, while the other decided to hold about seven head on the opposite side. This practise is not on and they learned their lesson. Just as Ronnie was to touch down, the seven horses on one side wanted to join the main herd and broke loose and headed to join the others. Ronnie was very quick to react, and pulled the plane up missing the horses with the propeller and wheels just in the nick of time. He did catch one on the head with the right horizontal stabilizer and bent the aircraft practically in half. The entire fuselage was bent and Ronnie was so lucky to walk out of that one.

Later the Insurance boys and an Aircraft specialist arrived, jacked the plane around and straightened it out as good as possible put on a new section and stabilizer, bounced it up and down for ten minuets or so and flew it out. I was really something that everyone escaped unhurt, even the horse who was knocked head over heels, was feeding moments later. Just another day at Cold Fish Lake.

The fall was coming to a close, and I had to make a decision, if I was to remain with this outfit or not. I sure as hell did not like the way things had gone that year, nor did I like Howard Paish's constant backing the hired help that came out of the Iskut area. They would not have lasted one day on Garry Powell's outfit.

The whole crew was all in all great to work with and sure pulled their weight. One needed to cull a few that were more problems than they were worth that was all.

I stayed on that winter to look after the horses and what an experience that was. The weather had dropped to minus fifty-five below; the thermometer could only go that low and was of its mark. I do not think, that I have ever been in such a colder country than Hyland Post and Cold Fish Lake in mid winter. The horses were doing fine, they had the entire valley bottom to use as cover. They were well adapted to the area. Even the 22 new boys figured it all out, they were easy keepers.

I would take a snow mobile out with a sled full of pellets then drop them in the track that I had just made. It did not take the horses long to understand that the noise of the machine meant pellets. This supplement helped them through the winter, even though many did not even want this little attention, they preferred to stayed out in the remote parts of the valley.

This was my first real introduction to wolves, and there were plenty of them. Every time you made a trip with a snow machine, the machine track would be covered with wolf tracks on your return trip. They used the machine track as a highway and was much easier going than fighting the snow.

On these cold nights, the dogs at Hyland Post would stay right up against the cabin door for fear the wolves would get them. They would kill a dog in seconds and often walked right between the cabins trying to get one out in the open. One would hear the long slow howl and in the cold night, it was like a chorus. One wolf would set of another, and then the whole mountain would come alive. With good binoculars, you could see them all standing out on the runway at night. Sometimes there would be upwards of twenty in a pack.

There was a young man up there who stayed with me by the name of Rick. One fine morning when the temperature was well bellow fifty degrees bellow, his morning constitution called and he started for the outhouse. I had barely put a log in the wood heater, when he flew back in the cabin and said to get the gun, get the gun. Apparently he sat down in the outhouse, which was a double seater, and a large wolf head came up through the second hole. Here we were outside in our long johns waiting for the wolf to climb out of the outhouse. Rick shot the wolf. I told him that he would have to skin this one by himself.

We had radio contact with Cold fish Lake and somebody there had a wood chip from a power saw cause a bad infection. The only way up to Cold Fish was by skidoo, and nobody had ever done the trip in the winter.

I loaded up a small Élan Skidoo with snow shoes, gas and pulled a dog sled behind with a power saw more gas and some food. I was going to see if I could make it there in the dead of winter.

I left in the early morning and followed the Spatzizi up as far as I could, then I hit the saddle horse trail and followed it. There were lots of hills to climb, which I used the snowshoes on and unhooked the sled. I would then go back, and pull the sled up and get back on my way. There was a couple of times that I was a little worried, when I would hit a spring flowing into the Spatzizi and it was very thin ice. I knew if I ever went through, that would be the end of the machine and possibly me.

Anyway we made it to Cold Fish Lake and I was steaming with sweat after fighting drifts and timber for 12 miles. I had about 8 miles to go up the lake to camp, but for the mean time, I wanted to dry out a little and took my parka of. The sun was out, and the weather had warmed

up a little. While I was sitting on my machine worried if I had enough
gas to make camp, I heard a commotion, and here comes a moose out
of the timber with three wolves hung on too it. Several others were
right on his heels. They crossed the lake at the lower end, and went up
into the timber on the other side. I figured everything has to eat, and
fired my motor and went on up the lake to camp.

 When I arrived, they were glad to see me and we had to get his guy out
to a hospital and have his eye looked at. That first night in camp was
full of excitement. There was a red setter dog that belonged to
somebody there and he was put out to do his business before turning in
for the night. This dog did not want to go outside, and he was
physically thrown out. It was less than a minuet, and we heard a
commotion with dogs barking and dogs whelping. We opened the cabin
door, and saw this red setter streaking through the night from cabin to
cabin with a huge wolf hot on his heals. If the wolf could have got him
lined out, he would probably have got him down, but the red setter was
so fast on his feet, all the wolf could get was a mouthful of hair. This
dog was scared to death, and could not even hear our calls to come
here. The dog finally saw us, and ricocheted of the door trying to get in.
He almost broke my leg, he moved so fast.

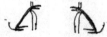

I held the lamp up while this other guy raised a rifle to shoot, he was
using the eye that was not his normal shooting eye, as it had a patch
over it and was covered. The wolf stood there thirty feet in front of the
cabin door while the first, second and third shots were fired. He did not
move one inch as the bullets hit right along side of him. The wolf was
totally disgusted about loosing the dog and left with a mouthful of red
hair.

This red setter had gobs of hair out of his sides and back end. He did
not stay out very long from then on when he needed to do his business.

The next day, another storm was brewing, and a small light plane
landed and he asked if he could spend the night and try again tomorrow
to make it through the mountains. All pilots were more than welcome
to stop over in bad weather. The next day I asked him if he would fly
me down to the other end of the lake and see if I could see any wolves.
I knew the moose was down someplace and wanted to see if I could
pick him out.

When we got to the end of Cold Fish, the moose had apparently come back out on the lake after I had left, and the wolves had killed him there, right out in the middle of the lake. I counted over twenty-five wolves all lying around the moose, with a few eating. When they heard the plane coming up the lake, they all ran for the timber. It was quite a sight seeing that many wolves in one pack. I noticed a pure while one that was a large adult wolf. The pilot then dropped me of at camp, and flew out; he was heading north, and must have made it through the mountains, because he never showed that evening.

Later, we were able to get a plane in, and the one guy was flown out to hospital to have his eye looked at.

I called Vancouver and asked Howard if he could send up some hunters to thin out a few wolves. There was a large pack that could use a little thinning. I went down to the end of the lake and there was still a lot of the moose left. I put four poles in the ground and left long streamers hanging from each one. I was hoping it would stop the wolves from cleaning it right up and hopefully thin a few out.

The hunters could not make it in due to bad weather and it looked like it was going to hang in there. I went down to the lake and pulled the streamers and poles down. It did not take but a couple of days, and they had him cleaned up.

It's amazing how wildlife always heads for water when threatened by wolves, unfortunately, they cannot figure out that in the winter, the lakes are frozen over and consequently loose the battle. I have witnessed several moose fighting wolves, if they would just stand their ground, they would have a better chance. That Nanny proved that, she weighed only 150 lbs compared to a moose that weighs in at about 1400 lbs.

I went back a couple of weeks later to Hyland Post and spring was almost here. At least in the lower part of the Spatzizi. There was one heck of a lot of snow left in the high country and would take a while longer to see any bare ground. We worked on the horses, and made it a point to round them up and hang bells on more and more as we caught them. Some of the neighbour's horses had joined ours, and we called him on the phone to come and get them. I believe there were about four head.

A young man by the name of Russ Kiersgard was sent up to collect them and he arrived and crossed the Spatzizi River. The best time to cross any river is in the early morning, or late in the evening when the river is at it's lowest. For some reason or other, Russ stayed until midday and said he was ready to take of with his horses back to the other camp at the lower end of the Spatzizi.

Several people told Russ not to cross, and to wait. He saddled his horse and led the rest that were all head and tailed together. The Spatzizi had come up a lot during the day with all the runoff and was very dangerous. Russ started across, and his horse lost his footing and down they went. All the horses came out on the other side except Russ. He made another mistake, and that was not shedding his heavy clothes and chaps. I don't believe they ever have found the youngster to this day. It was very sad and sure could have been avoided if he would have listened to everyone. We launched the riverboats and searched for several days. For many days around Hyland Post things were pretty grim.

I was going to give it a good try to see if things were going to change that coming fall, or if I was going to pack it in with the operation. After some serious thinking, I could see nothing was going to change, I decided to pack it in. I could tell, the handwriting was on the wall as far as how long the operation was going to last before it was turned into a park. I also believe the intention was to guide as many hunters as possible in the short time it had left. Howard Paish was quite upset that I was leaving.

When time came to fly out, there was no room for my gear and I both. All my gear had to stay behind and come out on the next flight. That gear never arrived in whole, several personal things seemed to disappear and nobody knew anything about it. All my gear had been gone through and several things pilfered.

Well, the Spatzizi was quite an experience and little did I know, that it was only the beginning, and a very large court case was to ensue between the Fish and Wildlife and the Spatzizi operation owned by Howard Paish.

It all came together several months later, when I was in Oregon.

I had received a phone call from a Wildlife officer by the name of Leo Van Tyne and he expressed a big interest in wanting to interview me with regards my involvement with the Spatzizi and Howard Paish.

I really did not want to get into any court case with the Game Department; it's members, politics or Howard. Only after several long talks with Van Tyne did he convince me to testify. The Game Department was questioning something about the lack of the necessary documentation with respect to certain heads that were en route to the lower mainland in a truck.

I guess things snowballed from there, and before I knew it, I was a instructed to appear as a witness for the Crown against Paish.

Not only was the Crown Charging him with several wildlife violations, but also with cruelty to animals over the packhorse that was left in the mountains. That was a very serious offence.

It was also evident that the Crown Prosecutor wanted to link several high officials in the Game Department for hunting in the area. For whatever reason they became involved in this case, I do not know. I tried to explain to everyone in court that while I was there, no special service was given to these men. They arrived in camp, and were dropped of in the mountains with only a bow, and were flown out after the trip. I do not believe they even shot anything. I do know they did not have any of our guides taking them through the mountains.

The day the court case took place; Howard Paish was quite surprised to see me as a Crown Witness. Court was held in Williams Lake and I never left the stand for two and a half days. The Crown Prosecutor was David Clarke and what a brilliant lawyer he was. I cannot remember all the charges, one thing for sure, the Crown wanted Howard and it seemed several others connected with him through the Fish and Wildlife. I wasn't interested in their problems. I said my piece and left. Clarke got a conviction on some charges, and it was all over.

The Spatzizi Provincial Park had been created, and I believe it also has the largest Ecological Reserve in Canada within its boundaries. It was a beautiful piece of the North and I am glad to see sections of the Province set aside for just that. It was called Spatzizi after the red colouring that the Goats would take on when laying in the soil and carbonate. The largest Goat herds that I have ever seen were up there. The most majestic sights with the Mountain Caribou and the vast herds were on the plateau. There were good sheep and fine moose and above all there were some healthy packs of wolves to keep everything in perspective. I was happy to see it take shape. It was a good place to make a park.

She's downhill and in the shade

CHAPTER FOURTEEN

Back to the Gathto

That fall I was back up at the Gathto River with Garry Powell. Roger my horse was not to eager to see me, but everyone else was. I had my first of five hunters looking at me, wondering what I was going to put him through.

Actually, there was nobody more than I that hated to climb a mountain for nothing. After years of hunting Stone and Bighorn Rams, your knees begin to hurt and you learn the mountains and areas a ram will prefer to hang out on and the ones he does not.

There could be a great looking mountain, and for some reason or other, the rams do not like it. Another thing I learned about Rams is that they are there like clockwork coming through a country Year after year they will use the same routes and almost to the day, you will find them the next year in the same area. There were plenty of Stone Sheep around. You are always looking for that forty incher. But you also never want to forget the saying, a thirty-eight incher down, is better than a forty incher on the other side of the mountain. I have lived by that rule all my life.

A nice Billy over looking the Muskwa

My Hunter with a nice Full Curl Stone Ram

Centre Picture is my heaviest Caribou that I ever got.

Hangars at Main Camp

Every hunter that I took out, got his ram, and in my entire Sheep hunting career I have only lost one ram. We hunted for him for three days, looking for scavengers and birds of prey. They would usually lead you to a dead animal, but it did not work.

I cannot to this day believe the ram made it out of the valley, but we sure could not pick him up. I would like to think, he was not hit all that bad.

From that day forth, I made it a point to ask my hunter to take several shots on his arrival to camp. I would make the excuse that sometimes the airlines shake the scopes. In fact, it was to see just how good a shot he is at a hundred, two hundred, and three hundred yards. I did ask a hunter once to take a five hundred yard shot. He had the calibre to do it and was a great shot. His name was Lloyd Ganton. I told him I would ask the Government to name the mountain after him. He laughed, but in fact the mountain just to the west was called Lloyd George. What a coincidence. When he came back the next year, I showed him the map, He could not believe his eyes, and to this day thinks it was named after him.

I have guided a lot of good hunters over the years, some sheep hunts really stand out and there is not a mountain that you pass without remembering exactly where you took a ram. This particular ram that Lloyd took was late in the season, and bad weather was always a problem, as the storms and cold could hit overnight.

I knew there was a very bad storm brewing from the temperature dropping.

We made a trip up to this one mountain, and the weather had worked to our advantage, as six large rams had moved down with the storm.

I told Lloyd this was going to be a last ditch effort to get a ram, as it was already starting to snow lightly.

Lloyd's Ram a fine full curl

**This Ram was the longest shot I have ever asked a hunter to take. It
was over 500 yards, and the last ram of the year**

Lloyd George Ganton's Goat

He cleaned the snow of a large boulder, and put his shell and coat down. Took a careful aim and pulled of a five hundred yard + shot.

The first two shots missed, but the third hit him and he dropped on this ledge. After the other rams moved up the ledge, he kicked and started to slide of the ledge right down within fifty yards of us. It was the last ram of the year, and had a very nice thick stone sheep cape. I have never asked a hunter to take that long of a shot. Usually its 100 to 200 yards of shooting. It's amazing how a sheep hunt can turn out. Just when you think everything is going well, disaster hits, and just as you think its all gloom and doom, things work out for the best. It has happened to me several times that when I was making a good stalk on some rams, for no reason whatsoever they started to move up the mountain. They were looking over our direction, but behind us, there would be a dozen or more Caribou moving down a trail. That movement was all it took for the rams to hightail it up the mountain and over, never to be seen again. If the Caribou had been within a few hundred yards of the rams, they would not likely have spooked, but they were just out of range, and not taking any chances.

Three very large and heavy Moose

Top Picture is Lloyd, his son, and his elk. Centre Picture is Grant Powell on the left and Doug Wiebe on the right. Two of the finest Sheep Guides that I ever worked with.

Some very nice stone rams with my hunters

It is always the big old ram that rules the roost. Keep an eye on him and the other younger Rams will most definitely wait for him to make the decision on when and where to go. I remember taking a large 38-inch stone with my hunter. The largest ram went and bedded down about fifty yards from the smaller ones. As long as we stayed out of his sight, we walked to within three hundred yards before all the younger rams bunched up. The larger one appeared by then, he knew something was wrong.

 It was all over as we were now within range and my hunter did not miss. I would not recommend anyone doing that, it could very easily backfire sometimes one feels lucky and the wind is in our favour. Especially if you have a hunter that is a good shot.

Over the years there are several Hunters that stand out along with some quite funny incidents that seem to find their way into a story. This one is about a school janitor from back New York way. The young fellow apparently had been saving his money to go on a Big Game Hunt. He was not an outdoor enthusiast nor had he ever hunted anything in his life. The kids in school had kidded him about this dream of his, saying things like "a grizzly bear will eat you" and the wildest things that can happen in the mountains. He was determined to prove to his school it could be done.

He arrived at Powell's and I was his guide. Not only had he never shot a rifle, he arrived with his boots in a box without the laces even on the boots. This guy was green as green could be. He told everyone in camp his story, and several of the other hunters were a little sceptical about even having him hunt with them. He paid the same price as everyone else, and would be treated no different.

The hunt began at Lower Prairie; from there we went to God's Little Acre where camp was set up. There were three hunters there, including the school janitor. The other two hunters were professional hunters that had hunted Africa and most places around the world. We were all going to try for a ram in the area. It was a difficult area to hunt sheep, as one could see twenty rams one time, and not another for the entire hunt. There was no alpine, and the rams were used to hanging on willowed ridges and small hills. Very unusual for a ram, but several large ones had come out of there, and we all thought it was worth a try. If it failed, we had time to move and pick up a ram in my other spots.

This hunter had the Luck of the Irish, because when he got his elk, it was slightly larger than the other two hunters elk. This went on through the caribou and moose. Everything was just an inch or two larger than the others.

US Federal Court Judge Walter Nixon and I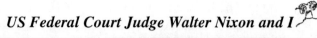

Bruno Shearer's Ram taken in Granny Creek

When he saw a large Black Bear, I explained that he had to shoot exactly the same way he did on all his other game. He fired the shot, the bear dropped, and the hunter turned to me and said," Gosh Chris, That's the biggest dam moose I have ever seen". His luck stayed with him through his Goat and Ram. All in all, he filled all his tags. I received a card thanking me for the memorable trip, and that he was hanging his gun and boots up. He said he only wanted to prove to the kids back at school that he was able to do it and survive. That was to be his one and only big game hunt.

 I wanted to send him back a card reminding him which way the heads were supposed to hang on his wall.

One of the most memorable hunts was with a hunter by the name of Phil Donato. He owned a brewery back East, and made thirteen days very enjoyable. I had always hunted Granny Creek; it really was my valley and always had nine or ten good rams in it. They were always in the same location. Every year that I would go in there, they were like clockwork, waiting for me. All the other guides stayed out of Granny creek.

 I watched this herd of rams for many years, and would take no more than two a year. They would always pick up rams coming through and the bunch never seemed to get smaller. Anyway, we spotted a very heavy ram in the bunch, he was boomed, but carried his thickness all the way through.

It took us four hours to make the stalk, and then we were in position, I was down on my belly sliding along a ledge. When I rounded the ledge, the big feller was right in front of us. He was lying on an outcrop no more than ten yards from me. The wind was blowing right in our faces, so he could not smell us. I asked Phil to get ready; he put a shell in the chamber slowly and stood up. The ram just got up and stood there totally dumfounded looking at us. Phil shot, and the ram ran about a hundred feet before collapsing on the hill. All the other rams just stood there totally lost without big brother. I have not to this day had a hunter shoot a ram closer than thirty feet. Personally, I would rather stay out there a hundred yards or so. Phil Donato went home a happy man. Not only did he get what he came for, we had a lot of happy moments doing it.

Me carrying out Dr Harry"Pusso" Morris's large moose from Samuel's mountain

188

Jack Powell with some nice racks in Lower Prairie

Me with a very nice Ram taken at the Forks

Mining Company Exploration moved out, and just left this entire camp at Granny Creek. It is an absolute environmental disgrace, as many drums of fuel are still there and will eventually leak. They should be made to clean their mess up. The Headwaters of Granny Creek is a sight for sore eyes when it comes to this mess.

Hy Erickson and his nice full curl Ram

Cam and myself, a very heavy seven/six point elk

Young Bull Moose breeding a Cow, with several Caribou looking on.
I waited an hour for this picture

Top Picture: two fine moose that Doug and grant got

Bottom Picture: Garry flying out of Samuel's Mountain. It took one heck of a pilot to do this.

My hunter Bruno Sheerer with his Goat.

Samuel's Mountain. The weather could change from sunny to minus ten overnight 🖐

She's downhill and in the shade

CHAPTER FIFTEEN

THE NORTH LOST A LEGAND

I was slowly starting to wind down all my Sheep Hunting up north for Gary. My knees were hurting from all the heavy loads and rams that I had carried out and all the spills that one takes in the rocks at night. Almost every Ram I took was shot the last few minuets of daylight. That meant preparing the cape and packing everything in the dark down to our horses.

I decided I would go up for one hunt a year and no more. That fall Gary called and asked me if I would come up for one hunt. I went up to guide the President of the Safari Club International. His name was Hy Erickson. He was and a great fellow to be with. We got our ram and goat in three days, we did a little fishing for a day or two and then we both left. The hunting season had only just begun; Gary thanked me for coming up, and paid me practically my whole falls wages for this one hunt.

Pete Cantrell on the left, Garry Powell centre with Phil Donato right 🖐

It wasn't very long after I got home, that I heard Gary had been killed in his plane. Apparently he was coming out with a load of meat and hit bad weather. He tried to land at several airports, and could not get down through the clouds. Finally, they tried to bring him in and he did not make it. I felt devastated and could not believe the news. It still hurts to think he died this way. To me he is the greatest Outfitter and Sheep Guide I have had the privilege of knowing, both as a friend and as a boss. After fourteen years of guiding for him and 73 stone rams later, we never had one harsh word.

Not only was he a remarkable person, he was a honourable person and one of the North's true Conservationists. You can credit this man for the Elks success in the Muskwa I doubt if the Elk in the Gathto or Muskwa River would have taken of like they did if it hadn't been for Garry Powell and people like him. He knew that without suitable habitat, no amount of protection could benefit any animal. Garry Powell gave the Elk the suitable habitat that was needed to get started, where and when they needed it most. Programmes now endorsed and practiced by the Ministry Of Environment.

Top: Garry and I after a Bighorn in Clinton BC

Bottom: Bighorn Ewes on the Fraser River

Two Hunters getting ready to leave base camp, and Garry Powell on the right

I owe a lot to this man; he let me be part of the finest run hunting operation in the North. There was no better game outside of the National Parks.

She's downhill and in the shade

CHAPTER SIXTEEN

THE MUSKWA

The Operation later sold and was called The Big Nine Outfitters. I did go back up the Muskwa River several years later and I also made a trip up to my old stomping ground in Granny Creek. I did not feel bad about hunting this area myself, nor did I owe anything to this new outfit and the new owners. My elegance was to Garry and nobody else.

As usual and like clockwork, seven large rams were waiting for me. I felt good carrying a backpack and it was all different than having a good old horse to carry my load. My knee held out and the hunt was a good one. I saluted Granny Creek and said my farewells; I knew this would be the last trip that I would ever make up here. It had always treated me right and over all those years, it had produced twenty-eight rams for me.

I really did enjoy running the Muskwa River with a jet boat. It can be a little tricky in places, but all in all. It's a pretty forgiving river. She can get pretty bony if you leave the trip out to the highway into the first week in October. Anything past that, and your boat could be there all winter.

Barry Cline From Clinton on the Muskwa

Samuels Mountain was not far away from my camp. I had spent many days on Samuels Mountain when I had worked for Garry. One fall, I took my hunter who was a dentist from Missouri and we hiked on down a ridge. From that point, we sat and waited for the sun to go down. There is a certain time of day, when the sun will reflect of the horns of a moose. From that vantage point at about six pm, we counted

Myself at Kelly Lake preparing to head up the Muskwa River.

twenty-seven racks of moose horns glittering in the sun. It was magnificent sight, as all moose were better than fifty-five inches. There were some big old bulls hanging out in the muskeg and along the slopes of Samuels. We picked up a large fifty-eight incher that evening. The work began, as we had to pack all we could up the ridge to camp. That night, and all the next day, it rained so much that day, it reminded me of a cow pissin on a flat rock.

Garry would fly the super cub into a real hair rising strip on Samuels. There was no room for error when one landed and took off. We spotted the rams a few days later, and before the sun had set, we had a nice full curl.

Elk had just started to move into that area, and we would hear the occasional bugle. Now some thirty-three years later, there are many elk in the area, and doing quite well.

One fall several years later, I brought my girlfriend up and my friend Doug. He was my local dentist and had always wanted to see the Muskwa. We camped close to the river and later took a small backpack and we climbed up to Samuels to look at some rams.

I was not too comfortable with leaving her all alone on the river, so I went back after one night. The next day when I returned, I noticed very large grizzly bear tracks all around her tent. He never came back, but sure did check it out that night. I quickly covered all the tracks so she would not see them. From then on, I took her with me. It was great trip, the fishing was super and the Muskwa was full of Dolly Varden and Bull trout. There were some rams, lots of elk around and moose running everywhere. It was also interesting to see several Grizzly tracks working the area. By now, several local hunters had been coming up the river with jet boats, and the river was becoming like a freeway. That year, I logged fifty-five different jet boats on the Muskwa. Several were swinging up the Tuchodi, but the bulk of the boats were on the Muskwa

It did not take many years for the elk herd to get larger, and span out into and over more and more area. The resident hunters had found the elk and boats and camps were all along the river. I remember flying with Garry back from Samuels mountain the fall of 1970 and we saw this strange thing on the muskwa. We circled and low and behold, it was a flat-bottomed plywood boat with an outboard jet motor on it. That was the first boat that we ever saw on the Muskwa. We circled it several times and went on back to camp. I think we decided it was some exploration crew doing some work. In fact, they were the first batch of hunters to challenge the river that we had encountered. The game over the years got pretty smart, and moved of the river, the ones that survived that is.

A person nowadays, has to work pretty hard for any quality game if you are going to hunt that area. Soon as they hear a motor or the jet noise from a riverboat, they are gone. The few Rams that used to hang out on Samuel's are long gone. They made the trip across from Ewe Mountain many years ago and just stayed on Samuels Mtn. That is where Garry got his 46 incher and the 43 incher was taken. I took several 36 inchers and a couple of thirty eights. I don't know what is left if any. I did see a small band of Ewes, and I sure hope they got together with a Ram or two.

. I have seen the best that the Gathto could ever produce. I doubt if it could have gotten any better than it was in the late sixty's or early seventy's. It was not uncommon to go out with your hunter, and see upwards of ten six pointers in a day. One did not have to be a professional with a bugle, as most of the elk would come to you with a simple bugle and even a whistle from the back of a horse. I remember Bugling three large six pointers in and right out on a large flat. They all stayed out there fighting amongst themselves, and even after we took the largest Bull, the other two stayed and fought on.

The best Jet Boat Man that I ever met on the Muskwa or any River for that matter was a Man from Ft St John by the name of Larry Noble. He was a master boatman with rapids and could read water like an Otter. We became good friends and he finally after many years got married to Garry Powell's daughter Rhee. She is a great gal; both in the outdoors and under the worst weather conditions one could ever expect a woman to endure. This gal never complained in the mountains, not that it would have done her any good, ha.

Really though, I saw her when it was thirty bellow in Goat Camp and she kept on cooking in a small tent like it was not a problem. A real early storm came in, and the temperature dropped to minus thirty in two days. Our hunters were from New York, and froze their butts of. If they could have caught the Concorde out that day, they would have.

Rhee is one of the toughest gals along with her sister Connie that I have ever worked with, both gals could ride and hunt with the best.

Packing out of Blue Lake 🤚

She's downhill and in the shade

CHAPTER SEVENTEEN

BIGHORNS AND THE FRASER RIVER

This is the home to the California Bighorn, they now have spanned out from Lillooet to the Sheep Creek Bridge near Williams Lake. Back in the early sixty's; they were concentrated in Churn Creek and the Junction on the forks of The Chilcotin and the Fraser River.

There was a very successful transplant from the Junction with a hundred head into the USA, they have done very well. It's amazing how Bighorns can multiply with good management. I used to enjoy sneaking up on the big rams when I was real young. It was a bit of a challenge to get to within fifty yards of a big old ram and say to him, that he had better watch himself in future. He would be dumfounded and stare at me for a few seconds before bolting out and not stopping for several miles. I was with two game wardens once and I had showed them some sheep. They wanted to move closer and get a better look at them. I told them to get behind these big rocks and to stay perfectly still.

I then called the rams, and about six rams and twenty-five ewes came right down the mountain to within fifty yards of us. They could not believe what they had seen.

There were some very large Bighorns taken of the Fraser River. I got to see several 40 inchrs and one 43-inch Bighorn taken down by the OK Ranch. Bert Grinder got he 43 incher in 1968 and a large 45 inch Bighorn was brought into Town to be caped. It had been run over by a gal down at Spence's Bridge and came up to Clinton to be taken care of. I do believe it is in Victoria over some ones desk in the Ministry Of Environment.

The large rams that I encountered over the years were up the Fraser from the Gang ranch. They seemed to drift out of the Junction and head down river. The Rams in Churn Creek always summered up on Red Mountain and Poison Mountain. Several of the larger ones never showed up there, and hung out in the little Basin and Big Basin.

One of my favourite spots to get a large ram was always just up Churn Creek from the little Basin in very rough country. If you moved through there very quietly without a large entourage of horses, you could run into a very nice ram.

I once had a professional photographer wanting to shoot a lot of film of the California Bighorns. He in turn sold the footage to Walt Disney and other buyers. We went up Churn Creek and filmed forty-five ewes and three very large rams. He got all the footage he needed, and had a lot of action shots with the rams fighting. I remember both of us well hid in the crags, and the camera was running. I pulled out a can of chewing tobacco, and through it in the air. We were at least four hundred yards away, and over twenty head immediately turned their heads to see what that was. One never wants to under estimate the eyesight of a mountain sheep. Later, I lived in a small place outside of Clinton at Arden Park. It was there from the kitchen while my friend Orval was doing dishes that six big rams walked out within two hundred yards of the kitchen. I slowly took aim, and had our meat for the winter. He just happened to be a full curl ram.

One fall day, I took my jet boat up the Fraser and spotted five large rams. They were tucked away in this canyon ledge and were quite content just staying there. They had a lot of feed, and would show themselves only in the early morning, and late in the evening. There was absolutely no way that I could even consider going after them

So the waiting game was on. It was the third day before they made their move down to the Fraser to get a drink. I was camped beside a tree on the other side; it was all over in minuets.

I learned that the Bighorns on the Fraser could go up to three days without water.

While I was up in Williams Lake one fall, visiting my good friend Paul Sissons. I was invited to a local party. Paul, a very good Taxidermist, lived just North of town.

I did not know but one or two people in the room, but I could tell that several people were dedicated outdoorsmen and all were sheep hunters of sort.

I was asked where I was from, and said 'the town of Clinton'. He asked me my name, and I said' it was Chris kind'. He then asked me if I had heard of a guy by the name of Cactus, who lived in Clinton. I said 'that I had'. He then went on to say that he had heard from the Game Department, that this Cactus fellow was responsible for all the Old Rams disappearing from the Junction, which is the band of sheep at the mouth of the Chilcotin and Fraser River.

My reply was that if the Game Department spent more time walking the ridges and hills in the Junction and less time pointing fingers they could solve the problem with a few Cougar Hounds. They would see that a lot of the Rams were going to half a dozen cougar, a situation that was definitely on the increase in the area.

What an absurd statement, all that just because I spent a good part of my life hunting sheep? Later that evening, he asked me how many rams had I hunted over the years. To upset his evening, I said, "do you mean the ones I can talk about, or the ones I can't."

Any way, I did have a most enjoyable visit with my good friend Paul Sissons, and it was always a pleasure to see him.

One evening while we were sitting alone in the living room, Paul had remembered that he needed to take a large cougar skin that was still frozen out of the freezer. The head had not been caped out, so it was just sitting all folded with this head on top.

Paul put it right by the big wood stove in his living room to thaw out for the morning. It was while we were just sitting in the room, and it was all very quite. His wife's very large cat came into the living room. He was going to his place on the couch that he slept on.

Let me describe this cat to you, he was obese, his routine was a path from his food dish to the couch, with an occasional stop at the litter box. On his way to the couch this evening, he passed the stove, and immediately stopped and let out this loud hissing noise as he saw this huge cougar head staring at him only a foot away.

This cat was petrified, yet was afraid to move. He had one leg up in the air, and hissing louder and louder. Paul's eyes were wide, and a big grin was on his face. I was trying all I could not to burst out laughing. Finally after several minuets the cats leg came down and ever so slowly, he eased a few inches away from the cougar head. It was at that time, when he felt he had his confidence up to move out.

I stomped both feet on the floor and made a loud noise. This cat jumped four feet into the air from a standing position, did a perfect pirouette and peed and pooped all over Paul and myself. When he came down he scratched the linoleum for some five seconds before he got some traction. Finally he did and bounced of two walls, and the aquarium never to show himself for a whole week.

Paul shouted at me and said 'Look what you did to me, what did you do that for, look at me' and went to the bathroom to clean himself. I don't think I have ever laughed so much in my life.

Paul spent a great deal of time with me, he showed me the correct way of mounting a Black Bear, and then let me do a large Grizzly it was beautiful when finished, and he even said that it was a good job. 🐾

She's downhill and in the shade

CHAPTER EIGHTEEN

MY TRAPLINE

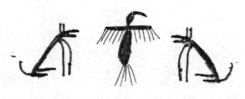

I moved back to Clinton and Got all the winter wood in. I worked on my snow mobile and got it all ready to do some trapping. Coyotes were a good price, and if a person could get a cat or two, it would really help out.

 I had about fifty sets made and there were coyotes everywhere. It did not take long, and the stretchers were full. There were some big coyotes that had rolled into the Kelly lake area, and there were a few cougar as well. I called several coyotes out onto Kelly Lake when it was frozen. With my 25.06 bull barrel, it could stretch out there quite well.

My trapline was quite large, and took in almost all the Limestone Mountains. For a Couple of winters I trapped out of the Circle H Ranch, which was half way from Clinton to Jesmond. There were some beaver in the creeks, but nothing one could make a living at, the price of beaver, just was not that good. My good friend Floyd Grinder was logging in that area, and I would make it a point to stop with my snow mobile and have lunch with him. It made for a good break. Also down at the other end of the valley was and old Indian called Eddie Grinder. He was a most remarkable person as older Indians are.

 The road was not open to his small log cabin which was situated well of the road. I would swing down that way, and have lunch with him and play a game of cribbage. Eddie was the fastest counter of cards in that game; he sure had a way with figures. I swear he could count faster than I could work a calculator.

I always relied on old Eddie to tell me the weather. This man was so accurate with the weather, I could not believe it. I always wondered how he could read the sky and be so accurate. He would look up into the sky, point here and there, mumble something and he would be right on five out of six times.

Then one day when I asked him, he just replied that he couldn't tell me. I asked him why? And he relied " that the batteries in his radio were not good anymore, and he could not get the weather report."

I had made several sets up in a draw and low and behold, I rounded a corner one morning and there was a large Lynx in the set. That helped get through the winter.

Twenty-two prime Coyotes going to market

I got about thirty coyotes that year. Trapping made the winter go a lot faster. It was at the Rabbit Farm, which was owned by Gabby Pilloud, he had Rabbits Running everywhere on his place. It was tucked away in the Mountain close to the Circle H. I had a set up on the power line, the set was for a coyote, but I had caught a cougar. It was a large cat judging from its tracks. I must have held it for a while, before he got loose. The set was an offset trap and easy for him to get out. He sure had the ground tore up. I have had little to do with cougars, my whole life; I believe I have only seen about six or seven in some twenty years. Then in one year, I must have run into at least ten.

Once, when I was stalking a large ram in a band of five, I was about seventy-five yards away, and four cougar ran no more than fifty yards away from me right into the rams and spooked them all. It was a female with her three young ones. The young ones were almost as big as her. She was teaching them to hunt. I wished she would have done it another time and with another ram. Neither she nor I got any meat.

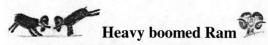

Heavy boomed Ram

My good friend Peter Newberry and our California Bighorn Rams

213

The Limestone Mountains out of Clinton

There was a ewe on the Fraser River that was near white in colour. It would throw a Lamb almost the same colour every year. Most years, it would be a ewe. Then, a few years later, I saw a white ram. I would watch this ram every year. He grew up to be a full curl and seemed to run in the same area. I thought this would be a real prize once he got older, never had I seen a white bighorn.

He virtually came right into my hands one day, and when the moment came, I could not pull the trigger. He stood in front of me and looked me straight in the eyes. His horns were about 37 inches and a nice full curl. I would estimate him to be about six years old. Hell, I watched him grow up from a lamb and remembered all the Indian stories about weather or not a person shoot the white buffalo.

I looked at him for a long time and I figured this guy was sacred to, if not that, he sure was special. I just watched him bound away down the draw. He was a real sight, and wished over the years I had taken some photos of him. He made it through the fall, but never showed the next spring.

I guess he fell prey to a big old cougar. There were several working that area that winter. I do see the occasional ewe that is a throwback to that old white ewe. There was quite a bit of white on this youngster also. I believe though the old girl only had one lamb that was a ram.

California Bighorn Sheep Country Where the White Ram used to live

My Jet sled that I ran the Fraser and the Muskwa with.

She's downhill and in the shade

CHAPTER NINETEEN
EMBER AND BO

I had to judge a rodeo in the small town of Bridge Lake. It was one of my favourite rodeos, because of its location, and all the interesting characters that seemed to come out of the woodwork once a year.

A man by the name of George Gammie approached me, and asked me if I could arrange for a cowboy to get on a bucking horse that he had brought to the rodeo. I told George that I did not think it was a problem, as the arena was full of them.

I asked around, and most of the cowboys were only there for their event and had to get on up the road for other rodeos. I figured I would wait and ask a local cowboy to get on him.

Before I knew it, the rodeo was over and I asked George if I could see the horse. We went over to his horse trailer and there standing tied up to the trailer was this grand looking black colt. He was very large and very well put together. Someplace in him, he had some good breeding. He said that the horse had been to five trainers and he had bucked with all of them. I asked George what he had to have for the colt. I believe it was six hundred dollars. We settled for a figure, and George delivered the colt. I called him Ember.

The work began with his groundwork. He breezed through that; obviously these trainers had done some of that.

When the time came for me to get on him, Put him in a small round corral and put my favourite hackamore on him. I could tell when my body hit the saddle, that he could not wait to get me in a position and cut loose with some gymnastics. Every time he even thought of it, I would drive his head into the logs on the round pen. And scold him with a few verbal bouquets. This work went on for several months; I would not have trusted him for one minute. It was just a question of time, before he wanted to test me. That day came, and it was a nip and tuck situation whether he got me, or I stayed on his back. Ember was fit and getting fitter with all the round pen work I had been doing. After a few minuets, he settled down and we resumed where we had left of.

Several months went by, and some friends came up to the area. It was Morley Short and all the Polo Team from Vancouver. They brought their horses out to Big Bar Ranch, they wanted to get their horses fit and legged up for the upcoming Polo season.

They asked me if I cared to join them on one of their long treks across Big Bar mountain and then to loop around Crows Bar and back to the ranch the. This called for some twenty-five miles of riding. I said that there was not a horse on the ranch that could do that at the pace these guys travelled. Then I thought of the big black horse called Ember. Why not, so I joined them and of we went.

The pace was fast and never did they slow down to a walk. It was trot and canter over hill and dale.

Slowly one by one all these polo horses were dropping back and after 15 miles, it was Morley's horse and Ember neck and neck. This black had more get up and go than any horse I had ridden. When we finally had the ranch in sight, Ember wanted to get into a canter. That was after twenty-five miles. This horse amazed me, because he was only a three year old. Morley asked me what breeding he was. I replied, that I had bought him from the Bridge Lake Rodeo and they were going to buck him. I did not know what his breeding was.

That was the day; Ember finally gave in to me. From then on, his schooling progressed rapidly.

I returned the next year to Bridge Lake and was flagging the field on him. A lot of people knew the reputation of this horse, and were quite

Ember the day he went with the Vancouver Polo Team.

Surprised to see him doing so well in the field and having centre stage at a rodeo. Ember was big, bold and black. He looked spectacular in the arena and behaved like a horse should. Very quite and obedient.

A person approached me and said that she had raised the colt and that he was in fact of Dutch Warm blood breeding, so now, I knew where Ember got his size. She also said that she had Embers Sire, and that she was competing with him in local Jumping Events. She asked if I would be interested in letting her take Ember and schooling him over some fences. I worked out something with her and Ember. Now he was being schooled in English tack and learning how to handle himself in closer quarters. The colt took to jumping like a duck took to water. He was very nice to work with and he learned how to control his pace and focus on the jumps and the course. Ember was very obedient and disciplined. He placed in several jumping events that season, and soon was to have a couple of mates.

Bo and Frosty would join him; it made for a nice combination of horses. Bo was a registered quarter horse. His name was Go Mister Bo Go and a grand son of the famous running horse Go Man Go. I had traded my Backhoe for him and liked everything about him. My good friend Doug White delivered Bo and loaded the backhoe. After several years of nice schooling, Both Bo and Ember turned out to be the two best horses that I have owned. Bo became equally as talented in jumping fences, but could never quite jump the higher fences like Ember. The nice thing about both horse, was that they were at home working cattle one day and In an English class the next.

One thing led to another, and the next thing I knew, I was purchasing a piece of property with this gal in the Westwold Valley. An old Thoroughbred facility was available, and had all the requirements for both raising foals and schooling horses.

All her horses and mine were moved on the property. I continued to work with colts and do some ferrier work with the local Thoroughbred Farms. Her stud was active breeding mares around the country and things seemed to be working out. I have to admit this gal had the patience and talent with schooling a horse on the flat, she had a very good seat over fences. The relationship was brief and lasted about two years.

I had acquired several other horses that I sure did like to work with and they all needed a new home. I purchased a property in my old town of

The Bronc Ember with Sandra and her baby

Frosty Springs. She was a Nice Mare who won several good races

"Bo Mr Bo Go" My favourite Horse. Equally at home winning a Jumping Competition or working Cattle

Ember over a Fence

Nice Collection with "BO"

Clinton. I asked my good friend and attorney Chad Mitchell If he could make who ever owned this property an offer. He laughed and said that he owned it. That worked really well for the horses and me. They had a nice three and a half acre spot with excellent footing, a nice riding ring; each horse had their own pens.

Ember with Police in Clinton

Frosty Springs at Clinton Rodeo

More and more horses were arriving and I was busy again. I had bought some very nice horses from my good friend Earl Blain. Earl was the leading trainer with all his Thoroughbreds for several years in the Province. He is still running a fine stable to date. He sure does know a class horse when he sees one, but relies a lot on his lovely wife Jeannie to make the major decisions and run the outfit.

I had just purchased a lovely gelding from Bill Barnes. Bill was the competition for Earl at the track and had some very nice horses. At the end of the race meet, I approached Bill and asked him if he would sell this one very well built thoroughbred by the name of Sherri's Knight. Sherri's Knight had won his last three starts but winter was approaching and so he sold him to me. I had a place for him with the others in Clinton.

He was going to be my new project horse, and could not wait to get started with him in the spring. The horse had the whole winter of. Come early spring, it was a beautiful day and I had just harrowed the

My new project horse "Sherri's Knight" winning his last race with Bill Barnes. He was a grand horse.

My Riding Ring in Clinton where I moved all the horses

228

Top Pic: Frosty Spring with Cool Halo Foal.

Centre Pic: "Bo"

Bottom Pic: The property In Westwold, B.C.

Ember leading the Parade with R.C.M.P. Police. Clinton BC

The Schooling area for the Horses

Large riding ring. I turned loose Sherri's Knight for a little romp. He went out there bucking and jumping all over the place. Then he stopped dead in his tracks and pointed his right foot straight out and went into shock. I could not believe my eyes. I thought he might have twisted something inside with all the jumping about. I immediately gave him some painkiller to settle him down. I called Earl and he came down right away. I called Garry Armstrong the best horse vet in the area and to look the situation over. Something major had happened internally, and all we could do was stop the pain.

I covered the horse up to keep him warm throughout the night, and was going to put him down within the hr if things did not improve. I went out to do just that, but he had died.

The next day Garry asked me not to bury the horse, because he wanted to do an autopsy to determine the cause of death.

Apparently, he had pulled a main artery into his lungs and there was no hope for him. It was a sad day for me, I really liked the horse, and he was such an athlete.

I had taken Frosty Springs to a top Thoroughbred Stallion to get bred. His name was Cool Halo and had proved himself on the racetrack. Frosty was due to foal and looked forward to seeing my investment. Before you knew it, there was another foal on the ground. And his called for another pen and shed to be built. Frosty was a very good broodmare; both Ember and Bo would not leave the foal out of their sights. Once the Mare had foaled, I needed a break.

I had decided to go on a brief holiday to Europe and spend a little time visiting the Island of Malta. My good friend Sharlene who was my neighbour in Clinton and someone you could relay on looked after the horses, and of I went to Europe.

I looked the horse situation over while I was there, and met this lovely lady. I had noticed the Mounted Police section over there, could sure use some schooling with their horses. I spent three weeks working with 22 Police officers and all their horses. I set op a programme for them to start working on all their horses' flexion. At least they would look a little better in parade work.

They asked if I would be interested in working with them and to draw up a resume to present to the Headquarters of the Police Department. Did they need schooling, the police themselves needed a lot of lessons, and we also needed a budget. This was a problem, because there was little or no money for this section of the Police.

I was asked by the Mounted section to evaluate and purchase five young horses for them. There was about thirty head of very nice Hungarian Bred Horses arrived for a Movie Film. Rather than take all the horses back to Hungary, I worked with all of them, and selected the best five. They were all quite large horses, with Leppizanner breeding in them. In fact, the department should have purchased several more of these horses, they were there on the island and ready to go.

In all other buying episodes, they had to go to Ireland and England for horses. Purchasing these would have saved them a lot of money with hauling and other expenses. Anyway, they had some new stock, and were happy.

I enjoyed the company of this lovely lady that I had met, and decided to spend more time out this way.

When I returned to Canada, I had thought about her more and more, and then I decided to sell everything and spend several months over there.

It was very hard for me to sell the horses. Both Ember and Bo had some six years of hard work on them with their schooling. Frosty had a nursing foal and was pregnant again with the World Champion. The property looked good, and that was it. Everything went.

I had a forty-foot container on its way to Europe. I purchased a nice little apartment near the ocean and was going to spend a few months working with horses over there. A good friend of mine by the name of David Hood asked me if I would give him lessons. He said that the exercise was very good for his hip replacement. I thought about it, and took David on. What we needed was a horse for him to learn on.

David was happy with flying to Northern Europe, and picking up a Warm blood or a Leppizanner. I recommended that we search Malta first, and see what we could come up with. There was not that good of a selection of horses on the island, but thought it better to check things out here first. A month later we decided on Max. He was a horse that had come out of North Africa and had arrived in Malta to pull Tourists around in a wagon. I guess Max did not like that too much with all the traffic, and so we purchased him as a saddle horse.

Other outside horses came fast and furious; every one on the island was sending me their problem horses. They were the most undisciplined horses that I have ever worked with. It's like everything and everywhere you go, people want to school their horses over fences, without doing any flatwork. They just don't seem to realize, that the good horses are made in the school and once they perfect their flatwork, they are then able to handle the course with ease. One can have a horse that is a real athlete, but if he cannot turn around in forty acres, he is of little use in a jumping competition.

I would drill them all in the school and work with them on collecting their horses. There were several very nice horses on the island and they did improve immensely with lessons. David was enjoying Max; he was a very forgiving horse. I would then work with him on his gymnastics preparing him for a small fence.

He loved the work and took to jumping very well. I worked with about twelve different people and their horses.

On a young horse over some small schooling fences in Malta

I also worked with several young colts. People over there had never seen a round pen to school a horse. Many horses did not have the flatwork needed to make a good horse.

This was one of the nicer horses that I worked with

Working with Students and their work on the Flat in Malta

In fact, they had never seen the things I would put a young horse through. I put only one demonstration on while I was there. It was done at the stables where we kept Max. I built a round pen out of stone blocks, as there are little or no trees over there. Some 250 people arrived to see me work three different horses. Two of them had quite a reputation on the island. There was nothing wrong with the horses; they were just smarter than their owners. One of these horses after a few months of lessons turned out to be a very nice jumping horse and carried himself very well on a course. David Hood decided to move to South Africa, and max was up for sale. He sold immediately to the top Polo player over there, he really like the horse. I asked the new owner at sale time if he would like me to work Max for him. He said that was not necessary, that he knew about the horse. He loaded him and was gone. I had Max so he could turn on a dime, and had a beautiful sliding stop. Something they had never seen before over there. We sold Max and made a nice profit. David got what he wanted, which was a lot of exercise for his bad hip and the Polo Player got one heck of a nice horse.

David even split the profit from Max with me, which I thought was a very nice gesture on his part. We had heard through the grapevine that Max was one of his top polo horses. Pretty good I would say. One day he's pulling a cart; a few months later he's a Polo Horse.

 The Mounted Police did not get the budget that was needed to inject some schooling into their horses and them. I had about had my fill of an Island that was sixteen miles long and twelve miles wide. I sometimes shake my head and say to myself what the hell was I doing over there anyway. All I can say is that it's amazing where a woman can lead a person.

One very interesting thing that I did get involved with while I was there was the Peking To Paris Classic Car Rally. Two Friends of mine called David Arrigo and Willie Caruana had asked me to be the stand in Co-Driver or Navigator for the rally. The entry for the event was a 1947 Ford Allard

I was present at the briefings and would be on call, if one of the two drivers got sick or injured and could not make the whole journey.

The vehicle was overhauled from head to foot before leaving in the container. Destination, The Great Wall of China. We tested the car for all kinks and problems on a trip across Sicily. It was quite an experience and met some very interesting characters in Palermo Sicily. We were advised to stay of one section of road in Sicily, because there were some bandits who would literally run you of the road and rob you. Believe me the mafia really does exist. It did not bother us, mainly because we had nothing to take. We were almost broke with repairs on the Allard, I did not know if we could even make it home.

Luckily we knew a very prominent person in Sicily who took absolute care of us with one call of a cell phone. We were picked up in a Tow truck vehicle. The Allard was loaded on another vehicle. Before we knew it, we were guests at his lovely home with some great Italian cooking. His name was Churmina. This man had the most beautiful artifacts recovered from sunken galleons around Sicily.

David continued on to North Africa to further put the Allard through its test, and I flew out of Genoa back to Malta. Now before I wrap up this Malta trip, I want to tell you about the most memorable hunt I have been involved with to date. 🖐

She's downhill and in the shade

Chapter Twenty

A Most Memorable Hunt in Malta.

A friend who had a shotgun Reloading Company in Malta invited me bird hunting. This sport was very popular on the island. The only problem was, that there were no birds to hunt. Whatever dared land on the island on its migratory route from North Africa to Europe stood a very good chance of not making it back into his flight plan. I had told nobody over there that guiding hunters had been a major part of my life.

So here we were about twenty locals all primed and ready, we travelled to Malta's sister island called Gozo. This island was not as large as Malta, but was much greener and a few very nice valleys, although not very long.

I noticed most everyone but us had a brand new Landover Discovery, Several people were wearing fancy designer Hunting and shooting clothes and practically everyone had a top of the line Berretta Shotgun. It was amazing the pomp that went into this event.

I was sitting in a covered area as a spectator, as I would not carry a gun. We heard a lot of chatter on the Motorola VHF's. The chatter began to increase, and I could feel tension in the air, something was going to happen. Everyone in the blind was excited and eyes were glued to the skies. As it turned out, a single dove had entered the valley from the west. He had just arrived from North Africa a hundred and twenty miles away; he obviously wanted to stop for a drink before heading on to Europe.

The Shotguns started to roar from the bottom of the valley. Shots after shots rang out, and echoed on up to us. It sounded like World War Two had started. I was informed the dove was headed our way and to keep our eyes sharp for movement on the horizon. The shotguns started again, and you could follow the route of the dove. The dove ran the gauntlet of those fine Beretta's then there was intensive talk on the Motorola's, as the dove had been hit.

Binoculars upon binoculars were brought out; the scanning of the valley began. He was spotted in a tree with a damaged wing. Hunters were dispatched to flush him out of the tree. Gun dogs were used and sent in first. The dove made one last attempt to take flight

and was brought down by three of the finest shots in the west. He was literally blown up and out of the valley by very expensive Berretta Shotguns. The dogs were sharp; they missed nothing and retrieved what was left of the dove. Not before giving him a little chew. The hunters were thrilled and complimented each other on their success. After all the hunts that I had been involved with over the years, this one took the prize.

I was considering having my picture taken with this group and bird for the record, but I declined. So ended my first and only hunt on the Island of Malta.

Just before I left the island, I got caught up in a terrible situation that had me sitting on the edge of my pants. I sometimes wonder how I get into these things. It involved my trusted friend, mining consultant, Oxford graduate, equestrian rider David Hood.

David and his lovely wife Jacqueline had a friend that lived on the Island. Her name was Maude. Maude was the daughter of a British Royal Naval Admiral and was retired in Malta and quite active, respected, and well known in the social scene on the island. She was an absolute darling. Maude had this nasty little dog that used to bite her and try to trip her as she was going down the long flights of steps in her house. We all were very concerned about this, as Maude was in her eighties and did not need this kind of treatment from a flea bitten mutt that had its teeth protruding from its gums like a piranha. Maude bless her soul had picked this stray up and given it the finest of food and the run of a lovely home.

Even though Maude knew something had to be done, she was reluctant about letting David and I take the dog to a new home. I had drawn a picture of her little mutt romping in the countryside and continuing to have a life of leisure. She finally let the little beast into out possession, where we promptly look it to the vet and had it put down. We then took the dog, and dumped it into a drum as far away as we could in the country.

Everything was fine for three days, and then the bomb was dropped. Maude wanted to see the dog for the last time and say a final farewell.

We were frantic for answers and we needed a solution to this situation that David had gotten me into. We decided on a plan. It was to tell Maude that just yesterday, her dog suffered a massive heart attack while playing with the other dogs. This story was relayed to Maude. She seemed to accept it, but insisted that she see the dog for the last time before we buried it.

Well you should have seen two grown men jump. I told David this was his problem, the best thing he could do was to go and fetch the dog and clean it up the best way he could.

After being in the hot sun for the past three days, this might be a little difficult. David did just that; he went looking into the country for a three-day-old dead dog.

I heard later he found the dog, washed and fluffed it up, made it look as decent and presentable as possible for Maude. Maude said her last farewells and so concluded a nightmare.

My stint in Malta was over. I said goodbye to some great people that I had met. I hope one day, we are all gathered once again around a nice campfire.

I was gladly on my way back home; the sandy beaches and intense heat could stay there. I was content with looking at a fast flowing river, the sound of an Elk bugle, that sweet smell of the alfalfa fields and pine forest something Malta has never heard of.

I returned to B.C and needed to be around my buddy's who thought I had deserted them. Several thought I was insane to begin with for going over there. All I can say is that it was an experience. I really did want to see the Mounted Police Get their budget and upgrade their standards. Maybe one day they will. They were very quick to learn and eager to show the public their horsemanship skills. Both in Regular Police Duties, Quadrille and Parade Functions.

My good Indian friends in BC. Dotti Jepp And Mike Rosette. I would go and stay with Dotti and her family on the Fraser River. Mike is my old sidekick from the Gang Ranch days, a real Horseman and Cowboy He lives in the mountains near the Canoe Creek Indian Reservation.

On my arrival in Oregon, I stayed with my good friends Orval McCormmach and Duff Severe. I was quickly reminded buy Orvals old girlfriend from Texas that the Rolex that I sold her several years earlier was not a real Rolex. Angie said that she now had a real Rolex on her wrist. Heck, I was sure it was a real one, I bought it for $55 dollars and the guy said it was real.

I made it to Pendleton in time for the very large annual horse sale in Hermiston Oregon. It was there, that I ran into my old friends from Canada Bud Stewart and Don Raffin. They were the auctioneers at the sale. We had some good old stories to reminisce on, some going back thirty years. Loren Wood was also there trying to steal a horse with a low bid. I mentioned to him that I thought he should repay me something like a bottle of good whiskey for that fine colt that I gave him at Empire valley some thirty-five years earlier. He just laughed and figured there was a statute of limitations on the time and whiskey. I never did get my bottle.

I saw an old friend who I had played a trick on for fifteen years. His name was George Hixon from Long Creek Oregon.

George was the worlds finest Mule Skinner, and could drive a team of twenty White mules in all the Rodeos and many Shows where they were called for. He sure knew how to handle mules, which is an art in itself.

Anyway, one day George called up to the Severe Bros Saddle Shop. Duff asked me to get the phone. I did, and George Hixon was on the other end. He had been drinking a little Whiskey and was quite loud matter of fact, he was down right rude.

He was asking who the hell he was talking to and using the most profane language known to man. I thought of the toughest Cowboy in Canada. It was a man called Gid Gardstead. Gid was a tall quite Bull rider who had two other brothers Mark and Dave. I told George Hixon that he was talking to Gid Gardstead, and I sure did not like the language he was using. George promptly told me where to go. I quietly told Mr George Hixon that I was looking forward to meeting him one day, and that I was going to kick his butt all the way to Long Creek when we did cross trails. I told George on the phone never to forget the name Gid Gardstead.

For years George would come to Pendleton and when he did, he would call the Saddle Shop. I was there to answer the phone. I recognized his voice immediately and promptly told him my name, which was now Gid Gardstead. I reminded him that we had a score to settle between us and it had to be settled. George in the mean time must have checked on who Gid was, and wanted no part of him.

Whenever I would ask where he was, and that I wanted to meet him. He replied that he was always over a hundred miles away buying cattle, and the phone reception was bad, and would have to cut.

In fact, he was down town wanting to come up to the saddle shop, but did not dare.

This went on for fifteen years, and every time he would call, it was his bad luck that he always got Gid Gardstead. In the year 2002 I finally told George the true story.

I had an opportunity to go down to a very historical ranch called the Vey Ranch. The ranch is owned and operated by an absolute darling of a lady called Marlyne Schiller. She is what you call a High Performance Woman. That is the kind that can go from very nice person to ballistic in 2.5 seconds. She raises some very nice young Quarter Horses. The main ranch is nestled in Butter Creek with its summer operation in the Blue Mountains. It is a magnificent ranch with two good airstrips in both its summer and winter range. Dick Johnson takes care of the main ranch and keeps all the women in line when all the cattle ans cowboys head up to the summer range.

The Manager and Cowboss is a young man by the name of John Hays Jr, we all call him Hayseed, But what a hand he is. John is always mounted on a good horse that his lovely wife Joan raised and probably broke. I camped with hayseed all fall, and got to work all his young colts and ride with him that year. I would have rather rode with his wife Joan than him. Guess you can't have everything in life.

His early morning breakfast was something to behold. He needed some instruction on adding some roughage to a meal. It was long into the afternoon, and I had told John that I was not able to go all day riding on just two biscuits and some gravy. He replied that he had not served me two biscuits for breakfast. There was in fact only one on my plate, it was in fact two halves and said," that I needed to loose some weight anyway". He said "that the colts were carrying too much of a load on their backs to begin with".

This one fall day, we were riding along with half a dozen cows in front of us. John has three very good Border collie's. One of the dogs unfortunately had to have a hind leg amputated due to a vehicle accident earlier in the year. Never the less, she has a big heart, and was back in the workforce after it healed. These old cows decided to turn and make a run for the bush. John dispatched the dogs to circle them and hold them.

This three-legged dog did just that, but would not come back when called; she was wrapped up in the excitement and did not hear him.

John rode up to his dogs and began screaming at the top of his voice for his dogs to "Get Back", "Get Back". My ears were ringing. I informed John that he need not continue shouting as his dogs had returned and were now by his horse's side. John kept it up, until he turned red in colour, and finally started to contort and twist his face and shake his head and neck. He stared of into space as though he was having a seizure and things went blank, he snapped, he tweaked. I asked John while he was in this mode, if he suffered from high blood pressure.

Without any hesitation, he reached into his shirt pocket and pulled out a card and promptly read that morning's blood pressure reading. Both the dogs and cows stopped, looked and listened, and carried on.

We discussed the nature of this serious situation once John came back to normal on the ride home I told John that he was going to have to control his feelings and emotions while driving cattle if he was going to live to be a ripe old age and see that old age pension. I also asked him if he noticed the face on the three-legged dog when he was screaming at her. He said, "that he had not". I said that the dog would actually smile at him every time he hollered. It was no doubt payback time for John having her leg amputated earlier that summer. John said, " He would pay more attention to his dogs and try to control his emotions on future roundups". We rode on.

*The Corrals at the Vey Ranch when they were built in the Forties. I
am currently rebuilding them all with equally large Tamaracks logs.*

It is nice to see large log corrals still used to sort cattle.

Cattle Roundup on Sheep Creek, Vey Ranch. Starkey Oregon

There are many good cowboys in this area that are always willing to help when called upon. To mention Pat Beers, Mike and Russ Evans along with Bobby Burrows and then there are two of the most colourful characters Troy Perkins and Garry Sewell. They are two of the great Team Ropers in the area and legends around Pendleton. Often they're helping evaluate various situations, looking for a good laugh and riding a fine horse.

Cowboys on the Vey Ranch Taken in 1943

Garry and Troy told me a story that I thought was pretty funny. Both of them were helping a local rancher roundup cattle one fall. Troy rode his horse over a hill into a remote section of the ranch. There was a car parked down on this dirt road. He waved to Garry to join him, and they both eased down on their horses to see what was going on. Maybe they thought they were broke down or something. Apparently the steam was building in the car, even though they had the windows down. The occupants were so busy fiddling around, that they never noticed two cowboys sitting on there horses only a few feet away.

The female occupant advised the male occupant that he had better not do anything like that, because she would get pregnant. He replied that he would be very careful and he promised her faithfully that he would be totally in control of his actions. As this scene and steam progressed, she hollered quite loudly that he was not able to control his actions, and to cease all further activities. She was getting nowhere with her demands. Troy could not stand it any more and shouted out to remind him that he made her a promise, and to stop now because a promise is a promise. The vehicle was immediately started and driven away.

Camping with these two cowboys sure makes for a great evening. Unfortunately my stomach is sore for several days after, all from laughing so much.

Troy Perkins on the left and Garry Sewell on the right

Both these Team Roping Horses sold for $25,000 and $50,000 each that's US Dollars not Canadian

I took the job of working with all the colts down there. They are a well-bred bunch of youngsters. There were about twelve in all, and a pleasure to school. The year is 2003 and looking forward to working with another crop of colts next year.

Picture of the Author Chris kind

I was at St Aloysius Gonzaga Boys School, my parents had sent me to a private school in the Island of Malta, both my parents were in the British Navy and had served in WW2 in Egypt and Malta, dad as an officer, and mum in the medical end. That is where I was born.

My father had a real soft spot for Malta. My mother bless her soul, longed for the wide-open spaces of Canada. I myself was hoping Canada would come sooner than later. I had lived in Canada since I was five years old; part of my schooling was in Canada, and the latter part in Malta.

St Aloysius was run by the Jesuits and in my final year, I was sent on a retreat into an old monastery of sort. I was not allowed to talk to anyone for three whole days the food was gruel. It was basically a recruiting process to see if I would be called for the Clergy.

On the third day, I was summoned by this one priest and asked if the Lord had spoken to me during this three-day ordeal. I said he had father. The priest was thrilled that he had, and asked me what the lord said. I replied that he had instructed me to quite specifically "saddle a fast horse and head West my son". He said "Head West for British Columbia, Canada as soon as possible". The priest was Fr Girlando he was one that I actually liked. He said, "that they're obviously is no chance of you wanting to be part of us". I said, "you got that very right Father Girlando." and that was the end of that.

In my final year at school, I had written to two Ranches, both were considered to be two of the largest and well-known operations in Canada; they were the Douglas Lake Cattle Company in Merritt British Colombia, and the Gang Ranch. The Gang Ranch answered my letter; Douglas Lake Cattle Company did not, maybe it got lost on somebody's desk. My final year at school was near and eagerly anticipated. I could not wait to catch a flight to Canada and then on to Clinton, British Columbia. It was the closest town to the Gang Ranch from the map I had studied so many times.

ISBN 141200037-8

9 781412 000376

Tony Veys Cowboys
at Jply valley - 1943

   I have known many a good Cowboy, Indian, outfitter, guide
and trapper along the trail. Not to mention several fine horses
that I rode and quite a few that bucked me off. This book is a
collection of events including all the fascinating characters that
have been a major part of my life since 1962.
I therefore dedicate this book to all the good hands that are
still out there pumping air, and those Great Ones that are not.
Wherever you are I hope the hunting is good and you are
mounted on a fine horse.
   May your ride from here on out be down hill and in the shade.

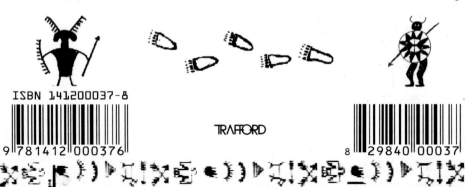

ISBN 141200037-8

TRAFFORD

9 781412 000376

8 29840 00037 3